APOLLINAIRE TO ARAGON

APOLLINAIRE TO ARAGON

Thirty Modern French Poets

Translated with Introductory Essay

W. J. STRACHAN

METHUEN & CO. LTD., LONDON

36 Essex Street, Strand, W.C. 2

First published in 1948

CATALOGUE NO. 5040/U

THIS BOOK IS PRODUCED IN
COMPLETE CONFORMITY WITH THE
AUTHORIZED ECONOMY STANDARDS

PRINTED IN GREAT BRITAIN

CONTENTS

ACKNOWLEDGMENTS

BEFORE setting out a list of acknowledgments, I would like to record here my gratitude to the following for their personal encouragement during all the stages of this project: to Miss Nancy Cunard, whose help and advice since the first of these translations, that of Péguy, appeared in the Liberation issue of the *New Statesman*, has made so comprehensive a work possible; to Miss Cecily Mackworth for her interest and appreciation and for allowing me to use various translations done for her *Mirror of French Poetry* (Routledge) and the French section of *Transformation IV* (Lindsay Drummond); to John Cullen of Methuen's for his patience when difficulties have arisen and for many helpful suggestions.

Grateful acknowledgments are due to the editors of the following periodicals and books in which some of these translations first appeared: *The New Statesman, Tribune, France, Translation London* 1 *and* 2, *Transformation, The Adelphi, Outposts* (Howard Sergeant), *Modern Reading* (Reginald Moore), *The Mirror of French Verse*, and *Adam* (Miron Grindea).

Further, I would like to thank the French poets or their representatives who have allowed me to publish translations of their work, particularly the following who have written their personal appreciation: MM. Aragon, Claudel, Éluard, Pierre Emmanuel, Tristan Tzara, Luc Estang, Francis Carco, Léon Moussinac, Francis Ponge, André Spire, François Mauriac and Saint-John Perse; the poet and publisher of *Poésie*, Pierre Seghers, for his valuable co-operation; and the critic, M. René Berthelé, for certain items of biographical information, kindly passed on by the British Council in Paris.

Thanks and acknowledgments are also due to French publishers and editors for permission to translate poems from books and periodicals in which the work of the following poets has appeared: Guillaume Apollinaire, *Les Alcools, Calligrammes* (Gallimard); Louis Aragon, *Les Yeux d'Elsa* (*Horizon*—France Libre); Francis Carco, *Vers Retrouvés, La Bohème et Mon Cœur* (Albin Michel); Paul Claudel, *Les Nouvelles Littéraires*; Jean Cocteau, *Plain-Chant* (Gallimard); Tristan Derème, *La Verdure Dorée* (Emile-Paul); Pierre Emmanuel, *Jours de Colère, Poèmes à Hölderlin* (*Horizon*—France Libre); Paul Éluard, *Poésie Ininterrompue* (Gallimard), *Poésie* 45 and 46 (Ed. Pierre Seghers); Luc Estang, *Formes et Couleurs* No. 6 (Ed. André Held); Léon-Paul Fargue, *Poèmes* 1912 (Seghers); Benjamin Fondane, *Adam* (Ed. Miron Grindea); André Frénaud, *Poèmes de Brandebourg* (Seghers); Jean Giraudoux, *Anthologie des Poètes Nouveaux* (Simon Kra); Max Jacob, *Fontaine* No. 34 (Ed. Max-Pol Fouchet); Pierre Jean Jouve, *Fontaine* No. 43; François Mauriac, *Anthologie des Poètes Nouveaux* (Simon Kra); Henri Michaux, *La Nuit Remue* (Gallimard); Jacques Prévert, *Poésie* 44 ; Léon Moussinac, *Poésie* 45; Charles Péguy, *La Tapisserie de Notre-Dame* (Gallimard); Saint-John Perse, *Exil* (Gallimard); Patrice de la Tour du Pin (Robert Lafferet); Francis Ponge, *Formes et Couleurs*; Claude Roy, *Fontaine*, No. 31; André Spire, *Le Monde Libre* (New York); Jules Supervielle, *Le Forçat Innocent* (Gallimard): Jean Tardieu, *Panorama de la Jeune Poésie Française* (Robert Laffont); Henri Thomas, *L'Heure Nouvelle* (Robert Laffont); Tristan Tzara, *Une Route Seul Soleil* (Bibliothèque Française).

INDEX OF AUTHORS AND POEMS

NOTE.—The order is only roughly chronological. The important thing in such a collection seemed to be to group poets and poems rather by affinity.

b

Introduction

" La poésie n'est pas un refuge mais au contraire une base de départ."

THE translating of poetry being largely a matter of personal taste, it would be unreasonable to expect that a collection of translations from one pen should be equally representative of all kinds of poetry. I would, however, claim for this one a unity which is not entirely accidental. Roughly it covers that long period of turbulence and unrest (1914-45) which has been called 'the thirty years war'. It embraces many different 'genres'. The subject-matter and technical approach is greatly varied. There are poems rhymed and unrhymed, poems in regular and irregular rhythms, the long 'versets' of Claudel, the prose-poems of Michaux or Ponge. There are poems by catholics, there are poems by communists. But within all this variety, they have one thing in common. They are, to use a dangerous term, 'modern'. All are by poets who have been, and are, aware that in all arts immobility is fatal and that the slavish imitation of academic models results in stagnation, poets who in their poetry subscribe implicitly to the attitude expressed by Aragon in the preface to *Les Yeux d'Elsa*, "il n'y a poésie qu'autant qu'il y a méditation sur le langage, et à chaque pas réinvention de ce langage. Ce qui implique de briser les cadres fixes du langage, les régles de la grammaire, les lois de discours.

C'est bien ce qui a mené les poètes si loin dans le chemin de la liberté. . . ." Basically, it is an attitude to language, an acknowledgment that words are alive and must be treated as such, that progress in poetry as in other things must be by experiment, the lessons of trial and error. Furthermore many of them (one might mention Apollinaire, Tzara, Éluard and Aragon for example) have not only written good poems but have materially enlarged the scope of French poetry from the point of view both of technique and subject-matter.

Considerations other than alliterative fixed the title of this collection. With Apollinaire a new period began in French poetry and about him there will be more to say. Aragon is an example of that rare phenomenon, the good poet who is also the popular poet. I do not know what percentage of the French public reads poetry, except that, judging by the number of reviews and weeklies publishing good poems, I imagine it to be well over the one per cent. credited to the English public by a recent survey, but Aragon's *Crève-Cœur* and *Les Yeux d'Elsa* met with a reception usually reserved only for prose works such as Vercors' famous *Le Silence de la Mer*. Even allowing for Aragon's prestige as *the* poet of the Resistance, it was remarkable. His importance lies in the fact that without concessions to popular taste, he expressed in memorable verse the mood and temper of the time. Nor are all his poems in the general sense 'easy'; full of allusion, *jeux d'esprit*, unpunctuated, they have nevertheless by virtue of their singing quality an immediate appeal lacking in so much poetry where the logic is easier. It is a quality of which Aragon himself is fully aware. In a review of the poems of Gérard de Nerval he refers to this 'song' in poetry, "Ce chant. Ce mystérieux pouvoir d'écho, ce qui fait vibrer les verres sur la table, frissonner les insensibles. . . ."

It is obviously not the *only* kind of poetry any more than love at first sight is the only true love, but both are exhilarating when they occur. Audisio, himself a considerable poet, makes the following comment: "Poems must be doubly understood, that is to say by the *ear* and the understanding. . . . Aragon threw himself with verve into a universe of stanzas and rich rhymes which he rediscovered for the astonishing delectation of a vast public."

If Aragon tends to be known as *the* poet of the Resistance, another distinguished poet of the same generation, Paul Éluard, was no less its mouthpiece. But his poetry lacks the immediate appeal of Aragon's. It is the distillation of poetry; it is like the subtle caress of a Spring breeze; something of which one becomes aware. In form—though not logic—it has the simplicity of an art that conceals art. It is bare but never arid.

The poetry of the third equally known though considerably younger writer of the Resistance, Pierre Emmanuel, is completely different from that of Aragon and Éluard. Here the effect is cumulative; here are the frenzied, declamatory rhythms arrested at intervals by the striking image.

It is interesting to consider when comparing the poems of one's own or a foreign language to what extent the poems compared are conscious, intellectually organised pieces of work, and how far intuitive and the result of a partial surrender to the subconscious impulses. No poet, I suppose, writes wholly one kind or the other, but T. S. Eliot might be cited as an example of the first, Dylan Thomas of the second; in France, the late Paul Valéry and Henri Michaux. Michaux states his case uncompromisingly enough: "La seule ambition de faire un poème suffit à le tuer." Poets and critics who acknowledge the contribution of surrealism to the new poetry (and it has been said that if surrealism has done nothing else than give to the French language its purest poet, Paul Éluard, it would have been enough to justify the experiment) are anxious that they should not be dispossessed of the precious conquests poetry has made in the last twenty years. Robert Lebel, in an article in *Hémisphères* (No. 1), gives evidence of a reaction and notes with misgiving appeals made on every hand to present-day poets to delimit their frontiers. "Les signes de cette étrange nostalgie de la férule se multiplient jusqu'à l'obsession," he warns them. In the same number, printed side by side, are the diametrically opposed views of the old and the new attitude to poetry. The spokesman of the former, Roger Caillois, writes, "the poet should express consciously all he wants to say, neither more nor less . . . no suggestion, evocative images, no mystery." In a word, poetry should possess all the qualities one demands of prose, 'nudité, clarté, précision'. The other writer, André Breton, refers to the new conquests in poetry, invokes the great experimenters, Rimbaud, Lautréamont, Mallarmé ('of the Cou de Dés'), the most important symbolists (Maeterlinck and Saint-Pol Roux), the Apollinaire of the 'poèmes-conversations', and reiterates the opening of the famous *Manifeste du surréalisme*: "Le seul mot de liberté est tout ce qui m'exalte encore." These fears for the freedom of poetry are very understandable. Inevitably during a war or time of national crisis what the French have called 'poésie de circonstance' gains an enhanced value. It has the topicality of much war-art, tends overmuch towards mere reportage, and suffers in consequence or else goes to another extreme when, in the words of the critic Henri Hell, "under the pretext of reintroducing in poetry the rights of the heart and those of feelings common to all men, free rein is given to the most deplorable facility and the most hollow rhetoric. Poets have celebrated the ravaged homeland, grief of separation, hate of the invader, hope, lost liberty. They have uttered noble cries, often heart-rending. They have re-discovered a human lyricism which is the hymn of a whole nation." And yet it is precisely such lofty subjects that need the resources of the gifted and inspired poet. To few poets is it given to write a poem of the quality of W. B. Yeats' *An Irish Airman foresees his Death*, or of Aragon's *Nuit de Dunkerque*.

One sees the dangers of this 'poésie ouverte à tous', especially if one feels that poetry has by the very circumstances of its creation a certain inherent mystery. It is not a medium for literal transcription, for the conveyance of fact—though there *are* poems and good ones that have done this well just as there are many prose pieces which are virtually poems, both realms having a rather vague and undefined borderland. So one must be prepared for the language of impressionism, for symbol, for allusion, for overtones conscious or unconscious, for the poem that synthesises a spiritual experience (like the Quartets of T. S. Eliot), for the poem that by a process akin to that of cubism in the graphic arts presents and juxtaposes various aspects of a scene or experience (*Zone* of Apollinaire). Henri Hell in the course of a review writes: "the poet uses words in order to create within the language, a language of his own. . . ." The life of a poem rises from the continual struggle between the language and the mystery it encloses. No question of wilful obscurity. Poetry like music yields its whole message only to the patient, sympathetic, and tutored ear.

In this rapid survey of the period of French poetry from 1914 roughly to the present time, it will be best perhaps to consider the contemporary scene first. We are still witnessing the aftermath of the Resistance movement and Liberation and the names of many of its poets are fresh in our minds. It is remarkable that so many poems written (and the outburst of poetry seemed in direct proportion to the enemy's efforts to discourage it) transcend the immediacy of patriotic emotion and have a permanent value. One cannot forget the courageous editors and publishers who at considerable risk printed them. Outstanding among the reviews were *Poésie* (edited by Pierre Seghers and printed at Villeneuve-les-Avignons), *Fontaine* (edited by Max-Pol Fouchet, published at Algiers), *Confluences* (edited by Jean Prévost at Lyon), the *Cahiers du Sud* (Marseilles), the *Bibliothèque Française* (produced by the Comité National des Écrivains and issued from the Centre des Intellectuels at Toulouse). The latter published work by Aragon, Benda, Jean Cassou, Paul Éluard, René Laporte, François Mauriac, Léon Moussinac and Tristan Tzara, and in the previously mentioned reviews there appeared, among others, Pierre Emmanuel, Claude Roy, Max Jacob, Saint-John Perse, Patrice de la Tour du Pin, Éluard, Tardieu, Pierre Jean Jouve, and Henri Michaux. There were the famous *Editions de Minuit* which published clandestinely prose and poetry by French patriots such as the now well-known *Le Silence de la Mer*. A full account of Resistance writing would fill a book. Whether in France occupied or un-occupied, in Vichy or in German concentration camp, there was the same manifestation of the French spirit to meet the challenge of the so-called New Order. All over the world French men-of-letters rallied to combat the double attack on French civilisation; Pierre Jean Jouve writing from Switzerland, Jules Supervielle from South America, Breton and Saint-John Perse from the United States, to mention only four famous names. I have referred to poetry written behind barbed wire, and I have before me a roneo-ed 'cahier littéraire' which came from Stalag XIA containing work by Gaston Criel and André Frénaud and others less known who sang of "le ciel lourd et la chaîne des jours". That the production of poetry under these circumstances was as much the continuance of a way of life as an act of defiance is obvious to anyone who considers all the other proofs, such as the marvellous illustrated books produced during the Occupation, some of which were shown in the Exhibition at the National Gallery in 1945. Despite all difficulties, all repressions, the French clung to their sense of values. Many paid for this devotion with their lives, and among the poet-martyrs whose names will be remembered not only in France but wherever poetry is read and courage saluted, are those of Max Jacob, Saint-Pol Roux, Gabriel Péri, Jacques Decour, Robert Desnos, and Benjamin Fondane.

The sonnet *Paris Double Galère* by Charles Péguy, who died in 1914, was strangely prophetic of the days that lay ahead, and it was not surprising to see it reprinted in *La France Libre* of March 1944. Péguy, partly owing to the monumental work on him by Romain Rolland, is one of the poets who have found a new public. He was a fervent if unorthodox Catholic, a great lover of his own country, and a moving poet. He was one of the first poets deliberately to eschew 'poetic' language and poetic subjects though he was hardly a revolutionary.

Guillaume Apollinaire was. The greatest single influence on French poetry since Baudelaire, he might be said to have created a new vision. A vision which used the technique of cubism in the endeavour to embrace and dissect the life the poet saw around him. But there is none of the surgeon's knife about the dissections of Guillaume Apollinaire—true though it is that he was not squeamish about his subjects—one thinks sometimes of the prism that breaks up a hard unmeaning white light into the iridescence of the rainbow. For him everything was a subject for poetry. Where other poets had found miracles in nature, he found them in industrial life. The new inventions of the twentieth century filled him with an almost childish delight; note, for example, his attitude to the aeroplane in *Zone*. This outlook is accompanied by a language and idiom broadened and enriched to meet the poet's need. Images and phrases from everyday life, puns, play on words, new rhythms for the new genre 'the poème-conversation', juxtaposition of seemingly incongruous subjects. Such are the characteristics of his longer poems in *Les Alcools,* and the more eccentric *Calligrammes.* If in the latter he re-invented typographical conventions of his own, it is with the bursting of old shackles that one associates Apollinaire. Alongside the changes he introduced are features that go back to that other free-born poet Villon, echoes of whom can be heard, as Cecily Mackworth points out in an article, *Je Suis Guillaume Apollinaire,* in many shorter poems such as *Le Pont Mirabeau* in this collection. "Apollinaire's blood may have been Polish and Italian, but his voice was the voice of the French troubadours."

For the origins of this new outlook in poetry one must turn a backward glance to a group of poets of whom four, Mallarmé, Verlaine, Corbière, and Lautréamont, were born within five years of each other and the fifth, the precocious Rimbaud, a decade later. 'Les Cinq', as they have been called, have profoundly influenced the development of French poetry. Common to all of them was the spirit of adventure in which they approached the whole subject of poetry and their attitude to the French language. They shared Maupassant's horror of the cliché; they deplored the outworn currency of poetic language. Their outlook on the traditional verse-forms into which academic poets continued to pour their banalities reminds one of that of the famous architect Le Corbusier who over sketch drawings of well-known neo-classical buildings in Paris scrawled an explosive "Ce n'est pas de l'architecture—ce sont des *styles*!!" Poetry must be alive. They rejected the easy eloquence and smooth rhythms that had been handed down to them. They replaced the stereotyped vocabulary of verse by a process which Mallarmé called 'céder l'initiative aux mots'. Words were used not in customary combinations as can be seen and, one should add, heard, by reading Rimbaud's *Illuminations*. I take an example at random: the opening verse of *Honte*:

> Tant que la lame n'aura
> Pas coupé cette cervelle,
> Ce paquet blanc, vert et gras
> A vapeur jamais nouvelle. . . .

In the same book under the heading *Proses* are passages which anticipate the genre, the 'poème en prose', of Henri Michaux, of Saint-John Perse, of Francis Ponge. Lautréamont's *Chants de Maldoror* are in prose also, but this strange and extravagant precursor of surrealism has continued to exercise a powerful influence on the ears and minds of the more susceptible poets. All of this group emphasised the musical, the incantational, the evocative power of words. Mallarmé in his famous poem *Le Coup de Dé* used all the resources of typography to provide a kind of musical notation for a poem intended to be read aloud. Regarded in this light, it ceases to be the freak publication that many would have it be.

xx

This introduction is intended only to set the stage for the translations, and readers who are interested in the full story of recent French poetry, the symbolist disciples (Henri de Régnier, Jammes, Moréas), the neo-classics (Mazade, Pize, Maurras, etc.) must not expect to find it here. French literature seems to specialise in 'movements' or 'schools', which indicates on the whole that French writers rarely write in isolation like their English counterparts and are more interested in artistic theory. It is to my mind not unconnected with the free and easy café life of Paris. How many manifestos, how many 'sommaires' of literary and artistic periodicals have been drawn up on the tables of famous cafés like the Deux Magots or the Café de Flore?

Apollinaire and his disciples André Salmon and Max Jacob were inveterate Parisians. Salmon, Jacob, Carco, and Derème were four of the so-called 'fantaisistes'. Their disrespect for bourgeois society was extended to its language, at which they delighted to cock a snook. Their poems aim above all at avoiding the self-conscious majesty of respectable but uninspired verse. They rejoiced in colloquialisms, *jeux de mots*, fanciful rhymes, witticisms of every sort, everything that served to debunk the high-seriousness of much 19th century poetry. They returned to the lighthearted manner of the 16th century. Behind this façade was something much deeper, and in the case of Max Jacob this gay mockery concealed, as time went on, a cynicism born of the disillusionment of the post-war period, but also a patriotic martyr's courage.

Apollinaire, after fighting through the war of 1914 and writing some of its best poetry, was to die in 1918 a victim of the Spanish influenza that followed in its wake. Meanwhile, in 1916, Tristan Tzara launched at Zurich the 'dadaïste' movement. André Breton, Aragon, and others met Tzara there. There were talks, lectures, demonstrations, writings round the new discovery. 'Dada' as a name for a movement which aimed at consciously destroying all academic standards in the arts and denying all systems and recognised values was chosen by the originator Tzara, who opened a dictionary at random and (aptly enough) found this word meaning a hobby-horse. It was a hobby-horse which before being ridden to death caused a good deal of stir in literary and artistic camps. The Dadaïsts produced, as one might expect, more than one manifesto. They issued reviews to which Apollinaire, vaguely on the edge of the movement and later to be rejected, contributed. Among artists associated with the movement were Picasso, Modigliani and Marinetti, a full account of whose activities is given in Wilenski's excellent book *Modern French Painters*. The movement had repercussions in Paris and to its review *Nord-Sud* contributed not only Apollinaire and Jacob but Breton and Aragon. The last two form a literary link with surrealism, which replaced dadaïsm. Less destructive in its outlook and with its programme of the development of the unconscious, surrealism has been more fruitful in art and literature than its predecessor. Apart from accredited surrealist works of art, the movement has had a profound influence on letters and art in France. Imaginative work was enriched by their exploitation of the unconscious, as it was by their technical approach (or lack of it), and it is significant that they invoked great writers of all countries, for example, Dante, Shakespeare, Poe, and Lautréamont. It is perhaps worth mentioning that Éluard, the modern poet who owes so much to this movement, has in his library the only extant manuscript poem written by the latter, who was one of their chief influences.

It is too soon to attempt to attach any label, even if one so desired, to French poets writing today. Most of them (and certainly all those represented here) are writing in the spirit and atmosphere of adventure that has pervaded French literature these thirty years. It is impossible to do more than indicate some of the characteristics of the new poets. I think one might say of them, as T. S. Eliot says of modern English poets, "what they have in common can be perceived by sensibility, but not defined in words". One is conscious of this new music in French poetry though its harmonies are various. The rhythms too: they may be made by the long swinging verset of Claudel, the slow sad chants of Supervielle, the psalmodic lines of Pierre Emmanuel. They may be the prose-rhythms, essentially poetical, of Michaux, Saint-John Perse or Spire. On each poem is stamped, as it should be, the personality of the creator. In some of the poets who have been writing longer, one perceives changes and development. But all those represented here, from the simplicity of Léon-Paul Fargue, that respected member of the older generation who associated himself with the Resistance in Paris, to Frénaud, who from his prison camp wrote movingly in a series of what Lescure has called 'unco-ordinated fragmentation', or that fertile inventor Jean Cocteau, have something which differentiates them from the symbolist movement which Apollinaire was the first to desert. Many names are absent, some unavoidably, but I hope there is enough here representative of the poetry of the present time to allay any fears and misgivings about the future of a neighbour to whose civilisation we owe so much, and which is so intimately bound up with our own. Our ears are attuned to a 'Chanson de Récréance'.

W. J. S.

Bishop's Stortford,
June 1946.

GUILLAUME APOLLINAIRE

Guillaume Apollinaire (1880-1918), born in Rome of Polish origin, found his spiritual home in France and above all in Paris. He was deeply affected by the poetry of Baudelaire though he reacted against the disillusionment expressed in Les Fleurs du Mal. *He is the exponent of 'cubism' in poetry and was intimately linked with the cubist painters, Picasso, Juan Gris, etc. He was also interested in negro art and the painter Douanier Rousseau whose seeming-ingenuous art has a resemblance to his own. He was wounded in the 1914 war, was trepanned but finally succumbed to the influenza epidemic of 1918.*

His most important work is contained in Les Alcools (1913) *and* Calligrammes (1918) *which have had a great influence on French poetry, opening up an unrestricted field of vision for the poets who followed him. Among other things he wrote a surrealist drama entitled* Les Mamelles de Tirésias.

Zone

You have grown weary of a world effete
This morning Eiffel-tower shepherdess your flocks of bridges
    bleat
Too long you have lived with Roman and Greek
Here even the cars seem pseudo-antique
Religion alone remains religion fresh-revealed
Simple like the hangars on a landing-field

Christ alone in Europe belongs not to ancient men
The most modern European is you Pope Pius Ten
And you whom windows watch and shame restrains
From entering a church to confess your sins
You read prospectus catalogue posters which shout in rows

This is your morning-poetry newspapers are your prose
Numbers at a penny full of crime-adventures
Portraits of the great and a thousand diverse features

This morning I saw a pretty street whose name I forget
Fresh and clean with the sun its voice was a trumpet
Directors workmen handsome shorthand-typists
From Monday morning to Saturday night four times daily
      tread this street
Each morning three times you hear the siren moan
And a crazy bell barks each day about noon
The inscriptions of the sign-boards and the walls
The plaques and notices like hoarse parrot-calls
I like the beauty of this industrial street
Situated in Paris between rue Aumont-Thiéville and
      avenue des Ternes
Once again the youthful street and you a little mite
Whom your Mother still keeps clothed in blue and white
You are very pious with your oldest friend René Dalize
Loving nothing so much as the Church's mysteries
It is nine o'clock the gas-jet lowered blue from the dormi-
      tory you steal
You will pray all night in the college chapel
While the eternal and adorable depth of amethyst
Turns for ever the flaming glory of Christ
It is the lovely lily before whose shrine we stand devout
It is the auburn-haired torch the wind cannot put out
It is the pale scarlet son of the Mater Dolorosa
It is the tree where prayers sprout ever closer
It is the double rood of honour and eternity
It is the star with six-fold ray
It is God who dies Friday and rises from the dead Sunday
It is Christ who soars better than airmen have soared
It is He who holds the world's altitude record
Pupil Christ of the eye
Twentieth pupil of the centuries He can do it alone
And changed into a bird this century mounts like Jesus to
      a throne

The devils in the pit raise their heads to peer
They say he is imitating Simon Magus of Judea
They shout if he can fly let us call him a '*fly*' one
The angels fly round the flying-trapeze-man
Icarus Elias Enoch Apollonius of Thyane
Hover around this first aeroplane
They divide sometimes for those borne by the Eucharist to
    clear the coast

Those priests who mount eternally elevating the Host
The aeroplane lands at last without folding its wings
The sky fills with millions of swallows this spectacle brings
Rapidly thither fly falcons owls crows
From Africa Ibis marabous flamingos
The Roc bird of whom poet-fabulists tell
Soars holding in its talons Adam's skull
As the eagle swoops from the sky-line its cry is heard
And from America comes the little humming-bird
From China have come the pihis on long supple feather
Their wing-span is one and they fly two together
Here is the dove the immaculate spirit
Lyre-bird and argus-eyed peacock escort it
The phoenix arising from its wing-fanned pyre
Veils all for a moment with its burning fire
The sirens leaving the perilous straits
Arrive all three singing gloriously in the heights
And eagle phoenix pihis of China and condor
Fraternise all with the Flying-wonder

You walk now in Paris all alone amid the throng
Herds of lowing buses near you glide along
The tortures of love your throat constrain
As if you were never to be loved again
If you lived of old in a monastery you would seek retreat
Now you are ashamed at the prayer you repeat

You rail and your laughter peals like a hellfire of sin
The sparks of your laughter gild the life within
It is a picture hanging on a gloomy gallery wall
Whose image at times you with closer eye recall
Today you walk in Paris where the women are dyed
    sanguine
It was though I would forget this it was beauty in decline
Surrounded with fervent flames Notre-Dame gazed up at
    Chartres
The blood of Sacré-cœur flooded me at Montmartre
The blessed words have robbed me of all ease
The love I suffer from is a shameful disease
And you survive sleepless and anguished in this image
    which possesses
You to whom so close it is this image which passes

Now I find you by the Mediterranean shore
Beneath the lime-trees all the year in flower
With some of your friends you take a boat out to sea
One is from Nice one from Mentone and two from La Turbie
We watch in a panic the octopus of the deep
Symbols of our Saviour the fish swim among the kelp

You are in the tavern-garden in the suburbs of Prague
You feel happy and a rose lies before you on the table
You observe instead of writing your tale in prose
The canker that lies in the heart of the rose

Terrified you see yourself pictured in the agate of Saint Vit
You were mortally sad when your eyes that image met
You are like Lazarus bewildered by the day
The clock-hands in the ghetto are moving the wrong way
And you retreat slowly into your life within
Going up to hear in the taverns at Hradchin

4

The peasants who sing an ancient Czech song
Here at Marseilles the melons among

Here at Coblenz Hôtel Géant your home

Here sitting under a Japanese medlar at Rome

Here at Amsterdam with one you deem lovely but is in
    truth an ugly maiden
She is destined to marry a student at Leyden
One can hire rooms in latin *Cubicula locanda*
I remember I spent three days there and as many at Gouda

Now in Paris before the judge they attest
While you as a criminal are under arrest
You have made journeys both grievous and happy
Before you were conscious of age and the lie
Of love at twenty and thirty you bitterly tasted
I have lived like a madman and my days were wasted
You dare no more behold your hands I can scarce restrain
    my tears
Over you over her I love over all that brought your fears

You watch with moistened eyes these poor emigrants
They believe in God they pray the mothers suckle their
    infants
They fill with their odour the Hall of Gare Saint-Lazare
As in the Wise Kings they have faith in their star
They hope to make money in the Argentine
And their fortune made back home enjoy their gain
A family removes an eiderdown as you would your heart
That eiderdown and our dreams are just as unreal
Some of the emigrants stay and find here a roof
In these hovels rue des Rosiers and rue des Écouffes

I have seen them often in the evening they take the air
    in the street
They move as rarely as pieces in chess
There are above all Jews whose wives in their pallor
And wearing wigs sit in the shop back-parlour

You stand against the bar with its filthy counter of zinc
Among the down-and-outs taking your simple drink

You are to be found in a big restaurant at night

These women are not bad and their burdens are not light
All have brought suffering to their lover even the worst
    'fright'
She is a policeman's daughter in the island of Jersey
Her hands which I have not seen are hard and creasy

I feel a great pity for the stitches of her belly

To a poor wench with a hideous laugh I now humiliate my
    lips

You are alone the morning will come
The milkmen clatter their milkcans in the street

Night moves off the loveliest of half-breeds
It is Ferdine the false or Leah attentive to my needs

And you drink this alcohol burning like your days
Your days that you drain like a dram to the lees
You walk towards Auteuil weary-footed wend home
Among your fetishes of Oceania and Guinea lie down
They are Christs of different form and faith
Each inferior Christ the false hope of a wraith

Farewell farewell

Sun so soon sunk

Pont Mirabeau

Beneath Pont Mirabeau flows the Seine
      And our loves too
Must ever there remain
Memory that joy succeeded pain
Though night must come the hour go by
The days move swiftly on not I

Hand clasped in hand and face to face we tarry
      While beneath
Our bridge of arms the O so weary
Waves of eternal glances hurry
Though night must come the hour go by
The days move swiftly on not I

Love like this running water goes
      Love also goes
Life how quiescent
Tormenting Hope how violent
Though night must come the hour go by
The days move swiftly on not I

Of days and weeks moves on the train
      And time that's gone
No former loves return again
Beneath Pont Mirabeau flows the Seine

Salome

If John the Baptist might but smile again
Sire I would dance better than all the seraphim
Tell me O Mother why your distress
By the Dauphin's side in the robe of a countess

At the sound of his words my heart beat O beat
As my limbs danced on the fennelled ground
And I embroidered lilies upon a banneret
That they might float on the top of his wand

And for whom would you now I did my embroidery
His wand blossomed forth on the banks of the Jordan
All the lilies King Herod when your soldiery
Bore it away withered in my garden

Come all with me beneath the grove of quince
Weep no more O pretty King's fool
Take this head for your bauble I bid you dance
Lay no hand on this brow Mother already so cool

Sire march halberdiers—march in their rows
We will dig it a hole for the earth to enclose
We will plant flowers and dance in a ring
Until the hour come when I my garter lose
His snuff-box the king
The infanta her rosary
The priest his breviary

Autumn

In the mist passes a knock-kneed countryman
With his bullock slowly in the mist of Autumn
That hides the poor and dismal hamlets

As he goes along I hear him hum
A song of love and infidelity
Telling of a ring and a heart that frets

Oh! Autumn autumn has made the Summer die
In the grey mist pass two grey silhouettes

Autumn Sick

Autumn sick that we adore
You will die when storm-winds in the
    rose-beds roar
When it has snowed
In the orchards

Poor Autumn
Die white and fecund
Where snow and ripened fruit abound
In the sky above
Sparrow-hawks plane
Over the dwarfs over the naiads whose
    hair is green
Who have known no love

By the distant wood
The stags have belled

And how I love your sounds O season
The fruits that fall unpicked
The winds and woods that weep
All their tears in autumn leaf by leaf

    The leaves
    We tread
    A train
    That sped
    Life
    That fled

Hunting Horns

Our history is the noble tragic
Mask of a king
No hazardous or magic
Drama no insignificant thing
Makes our love moving

And Thomas de Quincey drinking
His opium sweet and chaste
Of his poor Ann would wander thinking
Let us pass let us pass since all must pass
Oft will I backward turn

Memories are a hunting horn
Whose notes the wind effaced

Vendémiaire *

Men of the days to come remember me
I belonged to that epoch when sad and silently
Dying kings relinquished their estate
Were thrice courageous and rose three times great

How handsome Paris at September's close
Each night a vine-plant where the brightness grows
As of budding vine-shoots and above the town
Ripe stars are pecked where drunken birds have flown
And wait the harvest-dawn of my renown

One evening by the dim deserted quays
Returning to Auteuil I heard a voice
Singing gravely with now and then a pause
So that the river Seine might catch the plaint
Of other voices reaching clear yet faint

And long I hearkened to each tune and cry
The song that Paris roused nocturnally

For towns of France Europe the world I thirst
Flow down my throat till I am deep immersed

I saw that Paris drunken mid the vines
Was harvesting the sweetest grape that grew
Miracle-grapes that on the vine stalks crew

And Rennes replied with Quimper and with Vannes
Here we are Paris our houses everyman
Grapes of ourselves which sunlight did engender
A sacrifice to quench an avid wonder

* *Translator's note.*—First month of the French Republican Calendar, Sept.–Oct.

To you brains graveyards walls we bear
Cradles full of cries you will not hear
And from source to mouth our thoughts O rivers
The ears of our schools our hands clasped close in prayer
Our tapering-fingered hands the steeples soar
We offer too a mind of cunning store
That mystery closes as a house the door
That courteous mystery of loving-care
That fated mystery of other worlds the heir
Double reason which surpasses beauty
Unknown to ancient Greece and Orient
Double reason of Brittany where wave by wave
The western sea wears down a continent

Gaily respond the cities of the North

O Paris ourselves as living draughts we bring

The virile cities where hold forth and sing
The metallic saints of saintly factories
Our chimneys get with child the great-wombed cloud
As did of old Ixion mechanic proud
And these our own innumerable hands
Manufactories workshops hands
Where artisans naked like our fingers
Produce the real at such a rate per hour
That is our offering

And Lyons replied while the angels of Fourvières
Wove the heavens anew with silk of prayer
Unslake your thirst O Paris with divine words
That my lips the Rhône and Saône repeat
Ever the same cult from death arising still
Divides saints here and causes blood to spill

O happy rain O luke-warm drops O grief
A child watches the windows opening
And clustered heads to birds make offering

The towns of the Midi then made their reply

Paris the sole reason which can still defy
And fix our humour like your destiny
Mediterranean who withdraw your tread
Divide our bodies as they brake the bread
Their orphan dance exalted love-affairs
Will become O Paris the pure wine that endears

And a far-off sigh of death from Sicily
With a wing-beat intimates these words

Harvested is the fruit of our vine-field
And these clusters of dead whose heavy yield
Bear the blood-savour of the earth and salt
Take them for your thirst O Paris 'neath the vault
Obscured by clouds those pitiable bundles
Which Ixion oblique creator fondles
Of all Afric's crows at sea the cradle
O grapes and these dull eyes we find so homely
Future and life in these vine-stocks so weary

But where is the bright-eyed glance of the sirens
It fooled the sailors darlings of those dolls
But will turn no more on the Scylla shoals
Where sang three voices mellifluous serene

All at once the strait had changed its aspect
Faces of the flesh the water all
That can be thought on
Are but masks imposed on masked faces

14

He smiled young swimmer between the shores among
The drowned who floated in his wake
In close pursuit singers of plaintive songs

They bid adieu to abyss and reef in turn
To their pale lovers lying on the terrace
Then having fled to the all-consuming sun
Pursue them down to depths which stars embrace

When the night returned covered with open eyes
To wander where the hydra hissed this winter
And suddenly I heard your imperious voice
O Rome
With one curse my former thoughts condemn
And heaven where love directs the fates of men

The green shoots regrown on the tree of the cross
And even the flower-de-luce that dies in the Vatican
Dissolve in the wine I offer you which has
The pure blood-savour of the one who knows
Another and natural freedom which you fail
To acknowledge as the virtue all-supreme

On the floor beneath has fallen the papal crown
Hierarchs with sandalled feet now tread it down
O democratic splendour whose cheeks grow pale
When comes the royal night when beasts are slain
She-wolf and lamb the eagle with the dove
A host of royal kings hostile and cruel
Thirsty like you among the vine eternal
Will quit dark holes and mount into the sky
To drink a wine twofold millenary

15

Moselle and Rhine interflow in silence
It is Europe praying night and day at Coblenz
And I who tarried at Auteuil by the river
When the hours fell as vine-leaves shiver
And fall from the stock I heard the prayer recited
Which the limpidity of these streams united

O Paris the wine of your country is better than that
Which grows on our shores on the vine-stocks of the north

All the grapes have ripened for this terrible thirst
My bunches of strong men are bleeding in the press
You shall drink in long draughts all the blood of Europe
Because you are fine and you alone are noble
Because in you alone can God be realised
And all my vine-growers in these lovely houses
Which reflect in the evening their fires in our two streams
In these fine houses shown so clearly black and white
Blind to your reality to sing your fame unite
But our liquid hands clasped ready to pray
Lead to the salt water the streams that might stray
And the town between us as between the blades of
     scissors
Slumbering reflects no fire in her two mirrors
Of water though a far-off murmur hence
Disturbs in their sleep the girls of Coblenz

The towns were replying now in hundreds
I could no longer distinguish their distant words

And Trèves the ancient town
With their voices mingled its own

The whole universe concentrated in this wine
Which satisfied the ocean's animals each living thing
The cities the fates and the stars that sing
And the docile iron our good companion
The fire we must love as we love our own names
All the proud dead who beneath my brow are one
The lightning which illumines like a nascent thought
The names in sixes the numbers in ones
Kilograms of paper twisted like flames
And those above all who can bleach our bones
The good immortal lines which patiently grow bored
Armies ranged for battle
Forests of crosses my lacustrian dwellings
At the eyes' edge of one I love so much
Flowers leaving lips with cries
All that I cannot say
All that I shall never know
All everything changed into that pure wine
Paris thirsted for
Was proffered then to me

Fine deeds and days tormented sleep
Vegetation matings music eternal
Impulses adorations divine sorrow
Worlds which resemble you and resemble us
I have consumed you all but my thirst is still unquenched

Then at least I learned the savour of the universe

I am drunk with this draught of the universe
On the quay whence I saw the water flow and barges
    slumber
Hear me I am the throat of Paris
I shall drink again if it please me the universe

Hear my songs of universal drunkenness

And the night of September was slowly fulfilled
The red fires of the bridges were extinguished in the Seine
And as the stars faded day faintly rose again

Exiled Grace

Fade away O rainbow curves
Of charming colours iridescent
By your nature evanescent
Princess of the changing scarves

Rainbow into exile gone
Since exiled are sun's smiling rays
But a banner fluttering on
In the North-wind takes your place

Departure

And their faces were pale
In their sobs was distress.
Like pure-petalled snow
Or your hands beneath my kiss
Leaves of autumn fell.

Field Post-Card

As beneath this tent I write .
To you while summer evening dies
Where florescence dazzling white
Poised in the faint blue-tinted skies
Puffs from a bursting cannonade
Before they have existence fade

CHARLES PÉGUY

*Charles Péguy (1878-1914). A deeply mystical poet whose religion
was sincere but unorthodox. He broke away from the tradition of
the 'poetic' subject. His poetry is, in the best sense, national, cele-
brating the beauty and the spirit of his country.* He edited Les Cahiers
de la Quinzaine *from 1900 in which many famous names appear,
including his great admirer Romain Rolland. He was an early
casualty in the first world war. Two of his last works were* La
Tapisserie de Sainte-Geneviève (1913) *and* La Tapisserie de Notre-
Dame *the same year. In 1939 Gallimard published an anthology of
his prose and poetry under the title of* La France.

Paris Twin-Galleys

From time of swamp to perfumed Lebanon
Paris, twin-galleys, here at anchor rode;
And then through tale of palace come and gone,
Of private griefs, of glory spread abroad,
Of Roman Emperors, of Napoleon . . .
When our forefathers harnessed to the load,
Who kings had borne and thrice a people's throne,
Hung over slanting oars with shoulders bowed.

We, too, are chained to this, the well-worn seat,
With body, mind and soul must ply the oars,
Bent, broken, bruised but not effete,
Slave on these galleys here between her shores:
Our soul the phoenix rising from defeat,
Our body crouched by Notre-Dame's grey towers.

TRISTAN DERÈME

Tristan Derème, born 1889. *One of the same 'fantaisiste' group as Jacob and Salmon. His poetry has great exuberance but is not without a savour of irony. Among his works are* Le Poème des Chimères étranglées *and* La Verdure Dorée, *from which this poem is taken.*

And You Carco . . .

Pellerin, Vérane, Jean-Marc Bernard and you Carco
Who smoke a pipe and you who bend the bow
And pierce tigers and poems beneath the undergrowth
When the blue tobacco covers with its cloth
The leafage where wakes a tender nightingale,
Have you not dreamed of opening this parasol
Made of ostrich plumes and panther-skin
And naked, raising the vessel with its wine
Pouring before shops to folk standing agape
The intoxication of hillsides red beneath the grape
And in the midst of the street revealing to their view
The brown and black dogs and oxen and plough
The beige and blue jays, blackbirds singing to their mates
And a stream in the flowers beneath the gas-jets.

FRANCIS CARCO

Francis Carco, born 1886 *in Nova Scotia. Known chiefly for his novels but in his poetry is a typical 'fantaisiste'—full of wit and 'conceits'. One of his well-known collections of poems was* Chansons aigres-douces, *which dates back to* 1912. *A charming poem by him,* Chanson des Quatre Saisons, *appeared in* Nouvelles Littéraires *of January* 8, 1946, *Paris.*

Post-Cards

I

Though I address you from Bayonne,
My dear Tristan Derème,
Paris my heart is set upon
And my room by the banks of the Seine!

The Adour may bring along the blackened quays
A wave engendered by the Atlantic seas
And, far off, the sirens' shrill refrain!
But my ears are tuned to catch the cry
Raucous and plaintive under a grey sky
Of tiny tug-boats steaming up the Seine.

II

Here in Paris where I write
My dear Tristan Derème,
How I hate to see the Seine
In this drab and frosty light!

Chandernagor, Pondicherry
Than Paris make me feel less weary
And any girl on those native shores
Would seem a veritable fairy
Compared with these sophisticated whores! . . .

The Shadow

TO ANDRÉ ROUSSEAUX

When I waited for you in this bar
At nights, with drinkers quite far gone
Who leered so they might seem to laugh,
You had the air of being late,
Of fleeing from some one in the street.
Round you glanced before coming in,
Frightened; then closed the door again
But your ghost-shadow would always remain
Without, though ever in pursuit.

Your shadow is always in the street
Near the bar where I used to wait
        But you are dead,
And since, your ghost is there instead,
And when I leave, it is me it pursues
        Timidly like a hare,
        And if I stop, it stops there,
        If I speak, the shadow goes.

Your ghost is the colour of my lament,
The colour of rain, of time that is past.
It vanishes and is effaced
But in the dark is omnipresent.

Under the *Chapelle Métro* stair
In this noisy, insalubrious quarter
It waits for me, behind the black railing
With all its other fellow-ghosts,
To every passer-by appealing
With empty gestures of despair.

But the passers do not heed.
And—though the reason is never known—
In the draught that makes lights quiver,
In the cold draught a strange shiver
Follows where they have gone . . .
And I, who search where you may hide,
I who know you wait for me,
I pass but do not recognise . . .
All the night through I tramp in vain
Alone as in the former days,
And your shadow the colour of rain
Is blown by the wind at every stride;
And though it is swallowed in the dark,
I feel it always by my side. . . .

And you were only another whore,
A prostitute, if innocent-faced,
Like the one who gave a nod,
Standing in Whitechapel Road,
One night to Thomas de Quincey,
The one he sought but never traced
From house to house, from door to door . . .

He tells it in a book.

That was the time of our first chance-encounter;
Weary you were and sad, like the tarts of London,
Your hair preserving an acrid smell of fog.
And when they saw you by the bar-door saunter,
The drunken dockers made some coarse remark,
Or escorted you away, into the dark.

I have not forgotten the impression you made
In that despairing book,
Nor wind, nor rain, nor pavement-gleam,
Nor the look
Of murderers in the night,
Nor the public-house's light,
Nor the Thames' swirl
By the sad parapet . . .
It was many years yet
Before that other girl
So like you, was, by the grey slum
To beckon and accost me.

It is not you, it is all that you evoke:
How sad I was before we were acquainted,
How I burrowed snugly in my depression,
Walking up and down the streets, haunting the bars,
Bidding at night the shadows speak—
Always, always without remission
Condemned to walk . . .

But everywhere it was too late.
An accordion-tune wound up with a hiccough
And one by one the lamps were taken down;
The passer-by of whom I begged a light
Held out a dead cigar.
Wherever I dragged my steps, the same story,
Taking myself to where the trains whistled,
And on the great boulevard peopled with ghosts
I waited—for whom or what I did not know . . .
But the trains shrieked by
And this waiting seemed a departure.

You came only to go.
Yet I brought you to these lonely places.
You said to me: whatever happens
It will be always me you see among these shadows.
   I shall be close to you.
   You will think I am dead
   And never will you forget me.

I listened to you, I followed you under the sky,
Of living things we were alone
But I knew of the two of us which one
Would say goodbye.

To suppress the wish I tried in vain,
I longed to hold your slender hand—
The cry, the rumble, the smoke of the train,
The lines, the watchful beacon-flames,
The black bridge vibrating,
With the waggons' heavy clatter
By a dim presage—us already separating.

Another time in this unwholesome quarter,
We sat in darkness on a bench,
With the wind driving the rain,
The lights of boarding-houses;
Costers in wet sweaters,
Tarts eyeing us
Pressed on us like evil spirits
In an ever-narrowing circle.
   Then you began to weep
   To explain in quiet tones
   How one day you would bring relief,
   Free me from parasites within . . .

You spoke and the rain fell.
The rain had made you weep,
Like a sorrow that nothing drowns,
An unconsoled grief.

And the dance of the shadows and the lights of the houses
        Circled unceasingly
        With its toughs and tarts,
        Its bars and whining gramophones
        Hurling sometimes through the doors
        The appeal from a dead voice. . . .

        The dance that never wearied,
Turned and bore me away with you who are gone,
Turns and bears me again with all that was,
Beyond time, the world and all that therein is,
Or is not; but that you standing in the shadow, have
        known . . .

To Friendship

(These are the last two sections of a longer poem in La Bohème et
Mon Cœur *in which the poet has been recalling, in accents that evoke
the mood of Villon's* Où sont les neiges d'antan, *happy times spent in
the company of his fellow poets Jean Pellerin, Jean-Marc Bernard,
du Frenois, Paul-Jean Toulet. The last two figures in this poem are
probably of more interest to English readers, Guillaume Apollinaire**
and Alain Fournier, author of the famous novel with its boy-hero,
Le Grand Meaulnes, *of which recently a film version has been made.)*

"But in waiting my life has been spent!"
Groaned the Muse, with sly inflection.
"Waiting for whom and with what intent?"
But now the voice had more affection.

It seemed to say: "O Matelots!"
(I caught the accent of Monaco,
Mingled with laughter and tears)
And under his chevroned uniform,
And underneath that helm of leather
That bound his brow I could discover,
His eyes alight with malice gay,
Guillaume, my friend, whose funeral
Unhappily coincidental
Took place November, Armistice-day.*

"O matelots!" shouted the voice.
"O women sad, O matelots!"
Then, more dully, "Open, pray!"
Ghost, wandering in the land below,
Why do you cry to us and moan:
"And *you,* you had forgotten me!"

---

* *Translator's note.*—Apollinaire, after head-wounds received in the 1914
war, underwent the operation of trepanning.

To me, who O so dearly care,
Knowing we cannot lift the stone,
Alas, Guillaume Apollinaire,
That holds you, struggling, down.

A humble gate I have in mind
That creaked on hinges red with rust;
Where a decaying odour climbed
Over the top of a trellised wall
And dead leaves turn to dust,
And in the tree-tops, in thinning leaves,
A call, muffled, monotonous,
A solitary pigeon grieves . . .
Autumn was upon us.

I think of you, Alain Fournier.
O enchanted land of *Grand Meaulnes*,
Over woods and secret ways
The wind howls as in distant days,
In the story *Le Roi des Aulnes*,
We read in the first frosts.

No, death is not our common tie.
I see the same branch quiver and bend
Which quivered and finally came to rest
When this lad about to fly,
A timid creature, unexpressed,
—Such as we all have known
In the youthful years that are gone—
Suddenly let go the end
As he sees darkness descend.

Like a drunkard he took his flight
Your eyes watching him from afar . . .
Such as I see you in your books you are;
So to the pleasure of renewed delight
Under friendship's sign, that steadfast star.

Barbizon, 1936.

MAX JACOB

Max Jacob (1876-1944). One of the 'fantaisiste' group. Associated with Apollinaire and André Salmon. His poems show great wit and ingenuity, but in the posthumous edition of Cornet à Dés *behind all the eccentricities lies proof of a poet of genius. In his later years he was a convert to catholicism. During the Occupation he was put in a concentration camp by the Germans. He did not survive.*

Phèdre

Changed to a comet by bewilderment
Prayer, alas, falls but faltering from my lips
Returns to their utterer and strikes them, silent.

My hope a still-born grief pressed from these hips.
Your smile, Hippolytus, the executioner's blade,
With honeyed words its fall accompanied . . .
Dead or alive, who knows? I welcome death
Delivered from a god who holds my faith,
Be heedful of my eyes where Fate commands
At others' happiness I wring my hands.
Dead or alive? My carrion flesh that fed
Upon your guileless joy, now foul decayed!
My feet, my brow, the sky burns like a fever.
The being within insatiate for ever.
I move away with mantle to my lips
The beggars startle—let them shun my steps.
My way and path are nought but malady
All that lives or dies, all, all I vilify.
Swallowed the sword of love. The shots begin,
Have turned my body to a tiger-skin.
Plunge sword up to the hilt.
Despatch me then whose name is black with guilt.

LÉON-PAUL FARGUE

Léon-Paul Fargue, born 1878. One of the first poets to find poetry in modern aspects of life in the town. His poems about Paris have none of the sermonising so often found in urban poetry. He was in Paris during the Resistance. He developed the genre of the prose-poem.

On the Thread of the Pale Hour

One day, at dusk, we pass, after the rain
Skirting the parkside walls where dream the trees . . .
Long, long, we follow. The hour steals by
That night's deft fingers stitch upon the walls . . .
But what disturbs you in this pale thread of time
Hemmed to the hands, the black hands of the bars?
The dusk, the calm after the rain have somehow turned
Our dreams to exile and to night . . .

Now we hear the harmonious sigh
Of leaves around
As of a fire that takes . . .
And branches nod. Silence
Looks on
And scents so all-pervasive rise
That we forget that others can exist
For these would seem the scent of life itself . . .

Later a gleam of sunshine gilds
One leaf, then two then every one!
Then the first bird to venture forth
After the rain
Sings!
And as an acrid smell mounts from a deadened wick
So from my heart this offering of a dream . . .

34

A ray of light still lingers on the wall,
Slips from a quiet hand towards the shade . . .
Is it the rain? Is it the night?
Far-off some black and agèd steps
Move by
Along the parkside walls where old trees dream . . .

JEAN GIRAUDOUX

Jean Giraudoux (1882-1944). Like Claudel had an extensive political career and produced more in the way of novels and plays (a recent one being La Guerre de Troie n'aura pas lieu) *than poetry. Throughout his work there is a rich vein of poetry which glows through all the cynicism with which it is encrusted. The present poem is taken from* Suzanne et le Pacifique. *He was an ardent anti-Nazi and his death under mysterious circumstances seems to indicate their dislike of his independence. His last play was* Sodome et Gomorrhe, *produced during the Occupation.* Formes et Couleurs *reproduced a striking drawing of him by Jean Cocteau on his 'lit de mort', a drawing which brings out the extreme sensitiveness of his features which his works reflect.*

Suzanne and the Pacific

In London, the great town
Lives a being more alone
Than one shipwrecked on a reef
Than one dead his shroud beneath.
Great gaper, investor small.
Jeanne, that is his capital.

At Dover one of your eccentric fellows
Falls one day into the billows,
There he loudly calls for aid;
Clings on to a rock in the ground swell.
But no heart is thither swayed . . .
Adèle, thus dies the ne'er-do-well.

The great Chinaman of Lancaster
Lures you on with flower perfumes . . .
Then smokes you out with opium-fumes . .
Soon his pipe becomes your star!
To the poppy from the lily
The route, alas, is smooth, Cecily!

The Lord Provost of Edinburgh
Deems love to be a pack of lies.
But one day his Mother dies . . .
Down his cheeks the tears pour,
Irene the diminutive,
Love proves ever punitive.

In your exile what did you see?
Said Spencer to his wife at home.
At Vienna, Pergamo and at Rome,
At Calcutta? Nothing! . . . said he . . .
But the ocean beds to sound
Close your eyes, O Rosamund.

FRANÇOIS MAURIAC

François Mauriac, born 1885. Like Claudel, a catholic poet. More famous as a novelist and playwright. One of his plays, Asmodée, was an outstanding success in the late 'thirties. He has published a little verse which is of considerable interest and carries a particular tense atmosphere of its own reminiscent of that of the plays. Poems of his appeared clandestinely during the Occupation in Les Editions de Minuit.

Tartuffe

I prowl, a sultry storm, around your youth.
My lusts make in your sky brief glimmerings.
My glance despite evasive flutterings
Cannot escape the face of wounding truth.

With muffled steps, the look of sycophant
That age has taught the treachery of eyes,
Versed in the shame that years familiarise,
I prowl around a prey incognizant.

JULES SUPERVIELLE

Jules Supervielle, born 1884 *at Montevideo, studied in Paris, and travelled widely before settling down in South America. His poetry belongs to the kind that might be called, to use a phrase applied to some English poetry by Stephen Spender, "poetry for poetry's sake". Pierre Emmanuel, writing an open letter to Supervielle in* Poésie 45 (No. 24), *says, "Perhaps there is in every poet an infinite sadness which gives to our impermanence that pathos without which nothing permanent would be created. No one has been more aware of this than you. . . ."* *Among his works are :* Poèmes de L'Humour Triste (1919), Débarcadères (1922), Le Forçat Innocent, La Fable du Monde.

Saisir

Seize, seize the statue, the apple, the evening as it descends,
The shadow seize and the wall and where the street ends,

Seize the foot, the white neck of the woman asleep
And then open the hands.   How many birds escape

How many lost birds turn into the dapple
Of shadow, evening, street, wall, statue and apple.

Hands you will wear thin
At this serious play.
We shall cut you away clean
Of necessity, one day.

*   *   *

Great eyes in this face O who
Has placed you there?

Of what vessel mast-bare
Are you the crew?

By what raiding-party surprised
Do you await thus dazed
Open all night through?

Black gleams from a taffrail
Astonished but docile
Before storms that prevail.

Prisoners mirage-bound,
When midnight shall sound
Let your eyelids dip
To keep your courage up.

*   *   *

You were moving towards him, women of the vast plains
Sombre knot of desire, distances in the sun.

Suddenly your lips were frozen with hoar frost
When his slow face was advancing towards you.

You spoke, you spoke words ghostly and bare,
Reached out to him, cold words of a statue.

You made of this man a dwelling of stone,
A featureless façade blind day and night.

Can he not make a window in its walls,
A door so he may stir six steps abroad?

*   *   *

To seize when all escapes me,
And with what hands
To seize this thought
And with what hands
To seize hold of day
By the scruff of its neck,

Hold it quivering
Like a living hare?
Come, sleep, help me,
You shall seize for me
What I could not take,
Slumber of the mightier hands.

* * *

A face at my ear,
A mirror-face,
Comes and leans in the darkness,
"Handsome face, stay, have no fear,
Stay and watch.
It is a man and his sleep
That stand close beside you.
See that they plunge forward
In this thousand-league forest
Where leaves droop low
Like eyelids tight-pressed,
Terrain where the birds sing
Their songs under folded wing
And wake at dawn
To be silent and watch.

"Sleep, I listen and see
If the earth is still there
If the trees are still trees
If the routes still obey
And if the novitiate star
Which you discovered yesterday
Shines still in the smooth sky
And approaches our air.
Sleep while the houses
In their strength and their storeys

41

Tired of past glories
One moment disappear.

"Is it you that I hear
Through this great sleep,
White chain of mountains
Which divide me from you?
Am I on the old Earth
Where distances resemble
These lines of our hands,
No one knows who assembles?

"On each grass-blade, each stalk
On the quickest-moving fish,
I watch and I keep them for you,
I save them for tomorrow,
And you will find too
To disclose the world to you
Insects, the colour
Of eyes and the sound of time's music.
May sleep come and take you,
Already your bed remembers
Having once been a cradle.
May your hand open and release
Your strength and your weakness,
May your heart and your brain
Draw at last their curtains,
May your blood be appeased
And so favour the night."

Is it I . . .

Is it I still despite
This face discomposed
These limbs which take flight
In the dark silk of night
And this void of reason
Here where shutters are closed
And all the great stir
In this interior
And the luggage chosen
In the robbery she effected.

And what she neglected.

JEAN COCTEAU

Jean Cocteau, born 1892. *A brilliant individualist and experimenter from his early work* Le Cap de Bonne Espérance (1918). *He has enriched with his experiments the novel* (Les Enfants Terribles), *and the drama* (Orphée, La Machine Infernale, La Machine à Ecrire, *more recently* Antigone), *the film with his* La Belle et la Bête, *the ballet with* Parade (*in collaboration with Satie and Picasso*) *etc. The book from which this is taken is* Plain-Chant (1923).

Plain-Song

Poised to plunge beneath the waves of sleep
How hesitant you seem;
Perchance a fear that, following, I should keep
Close in your dream?

Fear not, for slumber differently embraces
My sleeping head,
And nightmare confuses you in childhood's places
With friends now dead.

While through the forests, meadows, farms you stride
On roads I love,
Locked in the heavy sleep wherein you hide
I never move.

Would that I might penetrate your dream
And tarry there.
But if the sun, rising, on you should stream
In searching glare!

PAUL CLAUDEL

*Paul Claudel, born 1868. Despite his work as a diplomat of high office,
he found time for the writing of many volumes of poetry. Some have
a devotional character, as their titles suggest:* Cinq Grandes Odes
suivies d'un Processionnal (1910), La Messe là-bas (1919). *He wrote
poems of the* 1914 *war which were justly famous. His essays on
anti-semitism were suppressed in the early days of the last war, and
during the Occupation. His poetry is characterised in form by the
long baroque versets.*

To Louis Gillet

Friend, from where you are, which is, I hope, Heaven, do
you remember our talks in Limbo and what they
meant?

Hamstrung we were and for the time that part unused
which in us hopes and is recalcitrant,

It was the time when—this country which long by habit
we have called our own,

Suddenly fallen beneath the horizon and this couch where
now we float strangely alone,—

Liberated from necessity, from weight, we talked the talk
of the survivor.

The past having acquired for us neither more nor less than
the present a foreign flavour.

A kind of funereal solemnity is upon us stronger than
bitterness.

The voice in the air rings strangely and these people whom
we touch invested with a posthumous grace!

Thus Dante when at the vague portals of Hell with Saladin
and Avicenna, he talked, the Florentine.

And it was precisely of Dante we were talking and of that
noble book over which he of your thought had passed
into mine.

We were discussing 'old man Satan' and that great chewer
of worms in the bowels of the earth both appalling and
naive.
Not the source of Evil and Hell, but in the ranks of the
other damned souls a kind of lodger and withal
inoffensive.
Milton, how much more penetrating his touch and how
much more tried!
"Evil be thou my Good!" exclaims this initiator of the
soul, everything which of itself deepens interest,
pleasure and pride.
The light lightens the darkness but the darkness would
have none at any cost.
Henceforth a whole literature and art which are distilled
in us solely from the poison of Paradise Lost.
Friend, what use were the world if there lacked some one
like you from time to time to look at it, to comprehend?
All these voices confused behind us, if there lacked some
one like you to unravel them and understand?
The formation of a style for example which to be used with
full ease
Has required so many men of every sort and period! hands
of all degrees.
First hesitation, then gradually the doctrine, the sudden
thrust! so much faith and so much to contrive,
That persistence in error which is just, borne by redeeming
fault to the masterpiece which will survive.
All these voices through time which though to each other
unknown, communicate,
All this future of which some one at the cost of a thousand
adjustments planned the fate,
All these consequences and all these contradictions all the
complementary lighting,
This proclamation with evidence and mystery uniting,

This secret of our heart of which some one ten centuries
    back and ten yards away from us is the trustee,

But to connect all this together and of it make a book, a
    picture all can see,

It needed through all time a man, tongues and all places
    and all time, a man who stands ward who can read
    and speak the interpretation

So that it may have sense and significance, viewpoint and
    direction.

A man deeply involved, each thing and each being who is
    there to bear witness, then what would he imply?

It is much more enthralling to listen to love him than to
    deny.

Although no rouged face, no wall beneath the plaster

But whose discoloration and cracks quickly proclaim
    disaster.

It is not only to the living, it is to the dead that I have
    something to bring.

It is at once on living and dead that I bestow charity,

And wash this face of theirs which is incapable of
    mortality

Whatever served no end, suddenly that has begun to
    sing.

And not only sing but this column in the full midday sun
    or this shapeless debris with bramble overgrown

Has elicited from us a response, has spoken to us in new
    accents as if for us alone!

Who shall say I have not done my task with true intent?

I have opened a way to the future and wedded past to
    present.

In the search for this sacred word which they had to form
    from one whole,

In thus linking together islands and continents I have
    achieved my goal.

Friend, it was in this strain we were conversing not many
    months ago on the bitter verge of grass.
The earth beneath our feet has ceased to belong to us, and
    this strange world around is painted as though on
    glass!

Brangues, le 24 Janvier 1944.

PIERRE JEAN JOUVE

Pierre Jean Jouve, born 1887. *In his expression of faith in people and sympathy for a suffering world he is very much a poet for our time. His poems have a religious background ; sometimes they seem remote. The nostalgia he expresses never degenerates into sentimentality, and his verse has always a distinction of utterance which has won for him the respect of the poets of the younger generation. First important poetic work*, Les Mystérieuses Noces (1925). *Among others :* Sueur de Sang (1935), Paradis Perdu (1942), Gloire (1944), La Vierge de Paris (1944), La Louange (1945).

Landscape of France

Timeless the castles plunge in the seascapes on the wall
Painting by Claude Lorrain haunted by golden haze,
Close to the corinthian piers I fix my gaze
Dazzled by the sights where ancient fanfares call.

Fanfares! all is calm and has been so an age,
This horizon of men and gods offers us peace,
Blue with tears and thoughts that linger by the quays
And the spirit embraces this sensuous cage.

Landscape of France! Did I know you of old,
Have the centuries lost me, do I still see you there
In my long day's exile between cold distant poles?

Or are you but an image they have hastily hung
In a time-honoured place whose track has been lost?

*   *   *

Lands where nature reigned
Beneath gold skies with sea-foam scattered
Wide horizons, on centuries' anvil battered
Lands immutable, unstained.

D   49

In the sun (washed are all the dead)
The rivers of architecture
Once again upright against his nature,
Man filling up the whole river-bed.

All is fine about him! and all he knows
Torments the breast of sorrow,
And freedom and light bestows.

His love to God's bitter cup
Returns, the world defeated
Where day is eaten up.

       *   *   *

As a teardrop to a fire
As a smile to a woman dead,
As a prayer is to the flood,
As a rainbow to the desert.

As pallor to the mind,
As a melody to frenzy,
As the soul to the burial-ground
As childhood to the rubbish-heap.

As the flame is to the hovel
As in chaos liberty
As laughter is to death throes,
As a raven to the forest.

PAUL ÉLUARD

Paul Éluard, born 1895. *One of the most distinguished of modern poets
who have used the technique of surrealism in their poetry. His poetry
is often quoted as an example of what has been called 'poésie pure'.
Poetry of this kind rarely has a popular appeal, though like that of
our Edith Sitwell it has a large following among a discerning public.
Recent work includes:* Choix de Poèmes, 1914-41, Poésie et Vérité
(1942), Poésie Intentionnelle, Poésie Involontaire, Au Rendez-vous
Allemand (1944), Poésie Ininterrompue (1945).

One Single Body

The heat has let loose
The forest bare
There is no forest more
No more journeys on the water
No faint shadow dimpling the thighs
The sky has become a burden
Our body a prey
Clad in ripened tears
Fingers are bleeding nails
Breasts turn on themselves
The lips lack all but sisters

There is no window more to open
There is no landscape more
Of air either fresh or foul
Our eyes revert to their source
Underneath the bare flesh of their natal beauty.

The Naked Land

The naked land
Where long I shall reside
Tender meadows has
Where your warmth reposes

Springs where your breasts
Mirror the day
Roads where your lips
To another's lips smile
Woods where the birds
Raise gently your eyelids
Beneath a sky reflected
By your cloudless brow

Sole universe of mine
Gift lightly accorded
To the rhythm of nature—
Your nakedness will endure

The Poet's Work

I

How fine to be with the others
On the worn turf in summer
Under white clouds

How fine to be with women
In a house grey and warm
Under a transparent sheet

How fine to be with oneself
Before the white page
Under the threat of impotence
Between two times two spaces

Between boredom and the passion for living

II

What have you come to take
In the accustomed room

A book that is never opened

What have you come to say
To her so indiscreet

What cannot be repeated

What have you come to see
In this place so unveiled

What the blind see

III

The road is short
Soon one has arrived
Where coloured are stones
Then
Hollow ones

Soon one has arrived
Where words are smooth
Words without weight
Then
Words void of sense

To speak with no message
Dawn is long passed
And it is not day
Nor is it night
Nothing—the echo of an endless step

The Age of Life

Notwithstanding stones
Shaped like men
We can laugh

Notwithstanding hearts
Tangled and mortal
We live on hope

Nothing makes us
Sleep without dreams
Suffer the shadow

There is not now
Suspicion or doubt

Of such an hour

Ever on earth
All moves and sings
Changes finds joy

Marc Chagall

I

Time was far-stretching history brief
The eternal mysteries gladdened the clock-makers
And children enumerated in chorus
The golden rules of reality

Rule golden-green rule yellow-gold
Rule golden-white rule of orange-gold
Of gold in the void of gold of gold in sterility
Day in day out with never a surprise

We the mad think of the rules of illusion
Rule of blue-gold and of black-gold
Rule of violet-gold
Golden rule of space

Golden rule that is frontierless
Rule nutritious and thirst-quenching
Erotic and infinite rule
Where the lips unwearying repeat the treasure

Marc Chagall

III

In my arms in my arms to laugh and to weep
My tears have the glow of your moistened lips
I set the world spinning round your pleasure
My garden is haloed round your face

We are the first to dream of flying
Together and the universe
Follows us as the float follows the hooked fish
But the light does not suffer

As you are the most beautiful and the most faithful
I am the most beautiful the most faithful also
Same fire from the same source
The same cool water in the storm

No windows but our windows
Whence life escapes where all things enter
Everywhere being the centre of love
Endlessly the first look

Our birth is perpetual

Note,—This poem is a poetic transcription of one of Chagall's pictures.

TRISTAN TZARA

Tristan Tzara, born 1896. *Roumanian by birth. He launched the dadaist movement in* 1916 (*see Introduction*) *at Zurich. He has always been in the forefront of causes for intellectual freedom. There is an obvious link between dadaism and surrealism, to which Tzara moved over. His most influential works have been possibly* Les Sept Manifestes Dada, *collected in* 1924. *Other important works :* 25 Poèmes (1918), Chemins des Étoiles, *which he dedicated to the Spanish Republican poet Lorca, shot during the civil war ;* La Fuite, *a dramatic poem* (1947). *The following poem comes from* Une Route Seul Soleil, *which was published during the Resistance period.*

The road has laid bare the ashes of misery
and the days I have seen the words that have passed
and the sun and myself chilled in inconstancy
anguish the most urgent love the most obscure
I stand on the world's rim a root which has strayed

pain has outstripped the end of the journey
in the solitude of towns linked with death we
by the seen threads and the unseen of memory
fearlessly open the flood-gates within us
and absent flow back heart-sick of lush pasture

forsaken ones on the majesty the silence of your pallets
I have learned the tongue of consanguinity
deaf indifference dream-gateways closed for ever
and the faintest glimmers where hung in the branches
belief in one's life half-dying on the road's edge

let respect find again its maternal straw
in the unnamed sorrows flayed without pity
the trees and the leaves suffice for tenderness
for no word is pure enough in all this brilliance
to cut through the diamond of their beauty around us

PIERRE EMMANUEL

Pierre Emmanuel, born 1916. One of the most prominent of the younger poets and a great anglophile. Became widely known as a poet during the Resistance period. His poetry shows considerable change and development already as can be seen by comparing the poems, for instance, from Jours de Colère *with later poems. Other works:* Christ aux Enfers (1942), Sodome (1943), La Colombe (1942). *Some included here are from a group entitled* Poèmes à Hölderlin, *published in* Horizon *in January* 1946.

To Federico Garcia Lorca

Column supporting the abyss! O shaft of glory
now split from your brittle night and stripped
of your bark even to the top—O memory
too naked for this murky dawn when fate
in smoke of horror thickened on the tombs—
you are white, your cry more shrill than steel
you sound for the hills alone in the sombre blue
you are the eternal lance in the heart of time,
the ear of corn which bursts through death, awakes
the word close-clenched between the teeth of the dead.
millions of swords stabbing the sea like blades,
cleaving the tuneless storm of bells, shattering
the sordid mirrors where the tyrants drink
lashing with foam the white cathedral flanks
whose lowered horns are goring out great furrows
of love, where the banner drips! where the blood wells.
The lark at sunrise dived down to the earth
to greet the dawn of the dead and crying root
the Tree sharpened in the wound which was the O
of Origin and Omega—the Word and empty
mouth delivered to the sad winds of dullness—

You may die: already the birds are hushed
already bleeds the abyss and space is lost
already Christ spills His Blood of future time
noble cypress! turned seven times in the wound,
(they are shooting you even now in your waste lands)
Granada is offered before you a prey to the worms
already the memory is hollowed out behind
the cross already planted sung and saved
your soul! you stand soulless alone with God
your soul bespattering the white wall of dawn.

Enchanted Sleep

Enchanted sleep chills the green vale
the sky has the simple colour of an old tale.
A castle haunts the air figuring Death
like a solitary cry heard over the heath.

Dead, eyes swimming with yellow flags and teal,
breast bare enhanced by blood on the brocade
she is forever queen in the splendour thus cruel
of white feet on the purple, the soul of a dagger blade.

A green-clad huntsman, pigeon held in his sights,
turns endlessly searching in the vast tomb-sky
that pure point where over the wound the bird will fly,
While on the black-canopied bed alights

Your gleam (clear mirror which crime conceals)
of pale gold between breasts where a rose congeals.

The Death of Hölderlin

Forty years you struggled with the shadow at your feet
before you were reconciled wholly with the earth:
shadowless at last. On you, nocturnal brow!
is read the depth of the stars. Your hands clasped
like two wounded turtle-doves embrace,
and turned towards the sea, your feet serene
repose long wandering. Your body glides away:
and pursuing bird, wings heavily to the shore,
face of a faultless blue remains alone
limitless noon where God sleeps 'neath the lids
(how naked the world is in these shuttered eyes!)
Above, the storm-clouds heap: the air alive
with bells, bright angels moving limbo-wards
the scent of hay rises from the threatened land
where the last gleaners hurry. On the road
the hearse of the pauper jerks between the fields.
A tomb bathed in the chirp of the cicadas,
lashed by the wind. Some crosses. Overgrown.
O the humblest of the humble. Just a few
pure hearts encircle you with silence.
The bell-tower weather-vane turns thrice
messenger of the clouds: but hardly
have you lain face bare within the tomb,
than the confusing beam touches your eyelids,
awaking the sealed-up sun beyond the grave.

LUC ESTANG

Luc Estang, born in Paris, November 11, 1911. *He is the literary critic of the Catholic daily,* La Croix. *Activity during the Occupation:* 'Adjoint' *to the Regional Headquarters for Limousin of the* National Front *movement, also member of the* 'department' *Committee of Liberation of Haute-Vienne, and member of the National Committee of Writers and of the National Committee of Clandestine Journalists. The poem* De Silence et D'Ombre *belongs to a series which will bear the title:* Prise du Temps. *Works:* Le Mystère Apprivoisé (*poems*), Invitation à la Poésie (*essay*), Les Béatitudes (*poems*), Le Passage du Seigneur (*essay*), Présence de Bernanos (*essay*).

Silence and Shadows

In that time—it was the time of shadows and silence—
It spoke in each word with strange dumb violence,
On the roads shadows fixed the passers-by at midday.
But at midnight eyes glowed in the thin threads of gloom,
And one caught in the word more than words used to say.

What tears shall steep the blood that blossomed on the
    tomb?

In that time—it was the time of silence and shadows—
That in vain over living and dead were extended
In vain heaped upon them the sand-grains of silence.
Their blood flamed—in the heart of the shadows contended
Their blood cried—a dumb song that echoed its resonance.

What flowers shall feel love in the newly-green meadows?

In that time—it was the time of shadows and silence—
Silence that set just and unjust in the balance.
Free-choice was enslaved and liberty slumbered.
But love came and voices and glow of men unnumbered

As men to live or die! in the silence and shadows.

LÉON MOUSSINAC

Léon Moussinac, born 1890. *His first poems were written at the Front in the First World War and published in the* Mercure de France *in* 1917. *He has always been associated with the theatre and cinema. He was, for instance, the editor of the periodical* Commœdia Illustré *and founded Le Ciné Club de France. He was a delegate of the 'Association of writers for the defence of Culture' and a contributor to the famous Communist paper* L'Humanité. *He was arrested in* 1940 *by Vichy and his health suffered during internment. Under the pseudonym of Jacques D'Aymé, he published poems in* Poésie, Fontaine, *etc., and under that of Lionel du Clos in clandestine publications. His poetry is characterised by a great sensitivity.*

Lament to be Sung

My friend on his round
crumples to the ground
his peril dire,
poor man as there are
so many to be found
at this second.

Why rates he less to-day
than yesterday?
O century of exile
of hate and of steel
if all your blood spill
will anything stay?

For nothing matters—
can that be true?—
as much as a secret.
Is there nothing but dies
but dies with regret?
The days are in tatters.

64

To wait breaks my spirit
but I cannot do other.
If of no merit
are love-song and lover
closed is my door
in silence for ever.

For Death I shall wait
on a stone and forlorn
bowing to fate
for happiness will—
said Bertrand de Born—
find me too late.

BENJAMIN FONDANE

Benjamin Fondane, born 1898. His poems appeared during his life in the literary reviews. During the last war, after languishing in the infamous Auschwitz concentration camp, he was sent to the gas-chambers of Birkenau in October 1944. Although he knew what his fate was to be he spent the previous evening composing a poem which he communicated to a friend who also was never seen again. These details were set down in a moving letter from André Montagne to Léon Moussinac. His Baudelaire et l'expérience du Gouffre *was published in 1947.*

Cradle Song of the Emigrant

The Queen said: See night dispose
   Her pearls on her breast
Pin upon mine a rose, a rose!
   —Wist, wist!
It is only a rose.

     It is the sound of the swell,
     sleep, sleep, little one.
     At dawn the redness will
     all have gone.

Good—said the Queen—O magic night!
   My shoes are not fast . . .
Already they dance by candle-light . . .
   Quick cobbler and last!
—He sleeps too by candle-light
   Leiba with his last.

     Sleep, sleep, little one!
     It is the shadows that play!
     While the wheels run
     Of destiny.

But what is this noise? The Queen said.
  I am dreaming of blood!
—It is the murmur at the springhead
  Fading in the wood.
Only the water at the springhead.

> A star flies
> to a new horizon
> tender and useless;
> sleep, sleep, little one.

A noise?—said the Queen—it cannot be so,
  Violent knocks!
—Only fowls they are training to go,
  game-cocks
To mingle their blood in the pit below.

> Sleep. After the squall
> the red-haired arc.
> It is the waves that lull
> the tiny shark.

O God—said the Queen—is it a decoy?
  that despairing cry?
—Only a slave in tears—a boy,
  for days gone by
in the flight of time he finds his joy.

> The dawn-sky is light,
> O child, make haste!
> See the strange white
> fish fly past.

Perhaps it is a soul that bleeds?
　　It is only some brat
　　—run—or too late!
lost quite lost as darkness spreads
　　break the spider's threads!

　　　　It is the sky that creaks,
　　　　it is God's night sky.
　　　　A province speaks
　　　　its malady!

Yet, this murmur of psalms!
Tallow candles, phantoms!
　　But who pursues?
　　—No, Queen, they are Jews
they are driving from the kingdom.

　　　　It is the wind's roar
　　　　the wild white horse.
　　　　It is the time when the hour
　　　　rings false.

Jews?—said the Queen—O what luck is mine!
　　And in my breath this catch!
It is surely no good sign.
　　Quick drop the latch
And then let me watch
my maintop-gallant-sail from over the Line!

CLAUDE ROY

Claude Roy, born 1915 in Paris. Sums up his life so far as follows:
'Travelled little. Always a soldier. Studied Law and Letters. Did
Journalism "pour gagner ma vie, poésie pour ne pas la perdre".'
L'Enfance de L'Art.

Bestiary of the Stars

Light O my light child
my little cloud awake
O drowsing joys
sweet friend my slumbering one
awake return
for while you are not here
through the lime-tree branches
through the garden-window
steals a star that flies and turns
familiarly
and settles lightly on your hand
softly without waking you
then a little strokes your hair
and goes as she has come
through the open window clear
with her child's barefoot tread
her gawky angel-heaviness

The star calls the whole sky
which skims around us humming
the thousand bees of night
tenderly despoil
your body's opened flowers
and your warm milky gleam
melts to the honey-maze of dusk

Altair and Denebola
rest on your neck
Betelgeuse and the Three Kings
drink from your hand
Celaeno and Meriope Orion
Antares and Procyon
are crouched against your thighs
Centaur and the Great Dog
are lying at your feet
and if I take you in my arms
I shall embrace the whole celestial heavens

My warm close-petalled pink
my fair bouquet of shade and flesh
between Mirab and Argo
you will rest till dawn
When the great gardener above
will cut his ripened fruits
re-gather all his flocks
set free his birds
who come to taste in turn
all that the vanished stars
have watched over by night
The nightingale and Oriole
replace the Gemini
but when you lift your eyelids
pressed close against your cheek
will linger a faint brightness
bearing a tang more salted than the day—
a memory of Perseus.

JEAN TARDIEU

Jean Tardieu, born 1903 *in the Jura.   Henri Thomas writes of his poetry 'the poetry of Tardieu seeks the object either in order to lose itself in it or to make a springboard of it and leap into personal solitude'.*   Accents, 1939.

Sleeping Love

As near to sleep perceptiveness abates
The body is a bell where still vibrates
Day with its cries, its sun which alternates.

But soon the universe has no access
Into this house of bronze and windowless
Where disembodied sound has found release.

It is an echo and to the morrow pointer,
The look exchanged as in a chance encounter,
The bird the hand set free for new adventure,

A lasting fire, a refined metal that bites
Into those caves where sleep leads me at nights,
Leaving a memory which dreams invites;

Two eyes are there, then gesture, voice begin,
Then a whole being with woods and meadows green
And cool, vast parks which I possess within.

What need have I to know so near my cell
Heart I imagine here beneath my bell,
Hearing the faultless rhythm of its peal!

The owls' wings will brush my cheeks in vain,
Break the night wind that nothing can restrain,
Tree crack and storm pour down its rain;

Dead and indifferent to the waves' despite,
I shall rescue from the scattered night
Only those things that give my thought delight.

PATRICE DE LA TOUR DU PIN

Patrice de la Tour du Pin, born 1911 in Paris. Catholic and mystic,
there is a certain kinship between him and Péguy. He is one of the
most promising of the younger poets. He was a prisoner of war in
Germany during the last war. His works include La Quête de Joie
(1933), Le Don de la Passion *(1937),* Psaumes *(1938),* Les Anges
(1939), Les Passants Tardifs *(1939). Also many poems written*
during the recent war which carry legendary overtones. His poetry
has a deep tenderness and musicality.

Death of Ullin

Erect upon his horse a knight—dead,
Portentous—steed slain in its last leap,
Clenched on the bit his hand steel-gauntletted.

Brutally roused from everlasting sleep,
Obliquely cut against the sky he stands,
Breathlessly panting from his long gallop.

His eyes bewitched me in their brilliance,
A secret sun wherewith archangels shine
And those who in eternal rhythm dance.

I whom the slow marsh fevers undermine,
One who would plunge to deep oblivion,
Or in the feckless mist of jingling line,

Before the prophet—noble name for one
Who drifts towards me as from a world beyond
Against a heart disgust has made its own—

I had deemed my soul a vagabond,
A beast hunted beneath the open skies
Such as one meets by some unfathomed pond . . .

. . . I am Prince Ullin whose heart arid lies,
Haunting at nights, possessed by demon sense,
Prodigious light that sweeps the far-off seas.

Now you must bid poetic mists go hence,
My rule will suffer no such compromise
Serving to obscure the final impotence.

Reading the dire, damnation-ridden skies,
I will teach you secrets that dwell therein,
The rhythm of Death itself and all its lies.

Your eyes seem fixed upon another scene—
As if a private passion you would hide:
Longings must go that thrusting intervene!

I promise you new worlds still scarce descried:
And when the others find your body fled
They will not take you for a suicide.

On the rising road by wisdom led
You will pass over Death's wide-open gate,
Bearing a lofty soul, on silence fed.

Hasten to quit the now outmoded set
Of legend, and climb heights nearer to the sky,
Shine in the body's incandescent light.

(Child of the solitude, I felt around me
The wind of fever blow, the tempest gather,
And heard the call of their anxiety.)

Yet we must go so little, little further . . .

HENRI THOMAS

Henri Thomas, born 1912 *in a village in the Vosges. He has made a name with his first poems in* Mesure (1939) *and* Travaux d'Aveugle (1941).

The Ladder

O with the world below the strange bond
by crazed eye, by trembling foot and hand

when the ladder, the sole ladder broken
—no one suspects my fall, and I awoken

stir, not too much surprised nor too defeated
sitting at the café, greeting, greeted,

with monstrous ladder-fragments mind is full
and everywhere I sow them, rung and rail,

a fragment here or there, that I have soon
the ladder entire extracted from my brain.

No sooner are you, my Jacob's ladder gone
And I resigned than you are born again!

And then my heart of every step takes count
again, again as to the Light I mount

Until Hell which lacks one child below,
remembering, shatters me with treacherous blow.

JACQUES PRÉVERT

Jacques Prévert, born in Paris 1900. *He is perhaps the last representative of an oral and popular tradition. His work has all the verve, violence and invective characteristic of a poet outside the academic tradition. He approaches his poetry writing in the same way as he approaches his work as a scenario-writer. Essentially he is an 'indépendant' working outside any school and has a large following among the younger men of letters. He had a notable success with the recent film* Les Enfants du Paradis. *He published in* 1946 Paroles, *a collection in one volume of poems, songs, stories.*

The Sultan

In the mountains of Kashmir
Lives the Sultan of Salamandragorum,
At dawn he dispatches many a head,
At nights retires with much decorum;
But in his nightmare lurk the dead
Who him consume,
And one night of all the number
He utters a great despairing cry,
And the executioner, roused from slumber,
Appears with swift servility.
"If no one were left alive,"
The Sultan said,
"There would be no dead."
The executioner replies, "O words of wisdom!"
"Then let the rest also succumb
And speak no more of them."
"O words of wisdom," the former said,
His phrases being limited.
And all as decreed go to their doom—
Women, children, his and others' kin,
The calf, the wolf, the wasp and gentle lamb,

The honest greybeard, sober camel of the plain,
Play-actresses, the beast of royal mane,
Banana-planters, makers of epigram,
And cocks and hens and eggs, eggshells and all
With no one left to give them burial.
"Like this, it's passable,"
Said the Sultan of Salamandragorum,
"But, executioner, you must stay
Here close to me
Ready to slay
ME if sleep should come!"

ROGER MOLINE

Roger Moline is a doctor by profession and one of the poets among non-professional writers who were stirred to write by events around them. He was a doctor in the Army but his normal work is in a Paris hospital and in private practice.

Homage to the Underground Press

The gods were dead, night-shadows veiled
The sky an abyss unlit by a gleam,
Thought was a crime and silence prevailed,
The night was the law and a tyrant supreme.

To thicken the darkness as days dragged along,
To stifle the lungs and the conscience that grieves,
On choking humanity to tighten the thong
Executioners donned their silken sleeves.

In a Europe enslaved played *petit caporal*
A jack-booted dwarf with his men black and brown,
'Interlopers', the word one had coined for them all
Who united all vices and scruples had none.

While we on the miracle hung, bated breath,
Its outlines receded, became dim and blurred;
But some found in shadowy oracles faith,
And others grew weary of hope ever deferred.

Then *Franc-tireur, France, Résistance, Combat* . . .
The underground Press—and the worst pessimist
Took comfort again as he saw from afar
Hope pursuing the clouds, heard the words: *We resist !*

ANDRÉ SPIRE

André Spire, born 1868 in Nancy. A Jew by birth and an inter-nationalist in the best sense (witness for instance the poem printed here). His poetry is characterised by the succession of rhythmic 'versets', a vehicle well suited to his subjects. Among his works are Poèmes Juifs (1919), Le Secret, Tentations, *etc.*

One Day

One day you will say:
Once I had a black girl.
Yeh, misses!
For I was born in the States,
When in Europe,
There was a tiger,
And a mighty lot of jackals after him.

You will say to them:
I had a black girl.
Not a white half-caste.
Perhaps a touch of brown,
With her face tilted upwards;
On her head, smooth, flat hair,
Dressed tiara-fashion, glistening with oil.
And when she passed in the sun,
Through her hair
Every rainbow colour glided.

We did somersaults on the lawn.
Yeh! like me she bent forward,
Put her head on the grass,
And flop!

And when I climbed on her belly,
Husky laughter
Gurgled and cascaded
And I felt each shake run over my skin.

She talked to the dishes in the kitchen,
To the grater, to the pots, to the bottles,
All of them came to life under her pink palms,
And filed into the cupboards
As under the passes of an enchanter's wand.
And my glass and my bowl
Rose to my pouting lips,
And sleep,
Upon my resisting eyes,
Fell, lulled by her crooning and the smile,
As from the lips of all Paradise's angels.

And why should it not have the smile of an angel,
The face of a black servant girl?
Is there not a black virgin at Chartres *
And on so many Byzantine mosaics.
And Balthazar who followed the star to the manger,
Was his face not as black
As the rock of Mount Moriah in Jerusalem?
And why should there not be a good God, black
With long hair,
Dark beard, ecstatic eyes
Like the Burne-Jones' *King Cophetua* in London,
Sitting at the feet of the little white servant-girl
With periwinkle eyes, whom he adored.

* *Translator's note.*—In one of the stained-glass windows. There is also a
statue of the Black Virgin in the north aisle.

SAINT-JOHN PERSE

Saint-John Perse, born 1889, *Guadeloupe. A distinguished diplomate.*
He was general secretary to the Minister for Foreign Affairs in 1940.
Wrote the very moving prose-poem Lettre à une Etrangère *during*
the war. His best-known work is Anabase. *Other works :* Eloges ;
Vents (1946); Exil (1943).

Snows

A Françoise-Renée Saint-Léger Léger

And then came the snows, the first snows of absence,
falling upon the great woven cloths of dreams and reality;
and with every affliction remitted to men of memory,
there came the freshness of clean sheets on our temples.
And it was in the morning, under the grey salt of dawn,
a little before the sixth hour, as in a haven of fortune, an
asylum of grace and mercy where the swarm of the great
odes of silence could be scattered.

And all the night, unknown to us, beneath that canopy
of feather, bearing its noble imprint and cure of souls, the
high towns of pumice-stone perforated by luminous insects
had not ceased to grow and excel, in the oblivion of their
weight.   And they alone knew something about it whose
memory is uncertain whose story aberrant.   The share that
the mind took in these conspicuous things, we do not know.

No one surprised, no one knew the first laying of that
silky hour on the loftiest brow of stone, the first touch of
that agile and very futile thing, the sweep as it were of
eyelashes.   On the bronze revetments and the out-thrusts
of chromium-plated steel, on the rubble of heavy porce-
lain, on the coarse-glass tiles, on the black-marble spindle
and on the white-metal spur, no one surprised, no one
tarnished it,

this mist of a breath at its birth, like the first fright of

F   81

a blade unsheathed . . . it was snowing and we shall tell
the wonder of it: dawn silent in its plumes, like a great
fabulous owl a prey to the winds of the spirit, puffed out
its white dahlia body. On all sides a miracle and a fête.
May grace alight on this terrace-slope where the Architect
showed to us one recent summer the eggs of a night-jar.

ANDRÉ FRÉNAUD

André Frénaud, born 1907 in Burgundy. One of the most original poets. He expresses himself with staccato violence. It has been said of him " la nécessité où il se trouve de désennoblir le langage rejoint celle plus profonde d'exprimer l'acte le plus simple qui soit et le plus nu . . ." Among his striking works are Les Mystères de Paris, Les Rois Mages, Poèmes de Brandebourg. *The latter, of which the one printed here is an example, were composed in a prison camp in Germany, the* Stalag XIA *referred to in the Introduction.*

Brandenburg

The Margrave of Brandenburg has made me sift sand
among the pines
for the heart of the Concrete-mixer
and my blood of cement beat even in my dreams
The great walls were lit up as the dawn arose
and at evening the birches stride off like flamingos
The stork has left the belfry of Quitzobel
and in its flight will pass over my ravaged country
—panoply of dead horses and tears
which have not yet ripened
to the pearl of our redemption—
above the life that awaits me
and which is dead
in Burgundy and in Paris
and Notre-Dame has turned towards me and smiled
she the eldest of our loves
I lean on my shovel
I am turned towards the setting sun
the sand slides off my face

FRANCIS PONGE

Francis Ponge, born 1899. *This poet has produced two collections,*
Douze Petits Écrits (1926) *and* Le Parti Pris des Choses (1942).
Some of his prose-poems have appeared in the periodicals Fontaine,
Poésie, Confluences, *and* Formes et Couleurs.

Fire and Ashes

Fire nimble, ashes inert.   Fire grimacing, ashes serene.
Fire simian, ashes feline.   Greek fire, Sabine ashes.   Fire
that climbs from branch to branch, ashes that descend and
accumulate.   Fire that rises, ashes that pile up.   Fire
shining, ashes dull.   Fire hissing, ashes silent.   Fire hot,
ashes cold.   Fire contagious, ashes conserving.   Fire red,
ashes grey.   Fire guilty, ashes victim.   Fire vanquishing,
ashes vanquished.   Fire feared, ashes pitied.   Fire bold,
ashes easily dispersed.   Fire indomitable, ashes that can be
swept away.   Fire playful, ashes serious.   Fire animal,
ashes mineral.   Fire irritable, ashes timorous.   Fire de-
molishing, ashes constructive.   Fire red and ashes grey
always in proximity, one of the favourite banners of nature.

HENRI MICHAUX

Henri Michaux, born 1899 *in Belgium. After a varied career in which he achieved a series of ambitions from being a Benedictine monk to being a sailor, he has lived mostly in Paris. He has travelled widely in equatorial America and Asia. Works:* Ecuador (1929), Un Barbare en Asie (1932), Plume (1937), Au Pays de la Magie (1942); *one of his latest works has been* Arbres des Tropiques, *illustrated with drawings by himself.*

Icebergs

Icebergs, unparapeted, ungirdled, where old dejected
cormorants and the souls of newly-drowned sailors
come and lean on the bewitching nights of the Far-north.

Icebergs, Icebergs, cultless cathedrals of eternal winter,
covered with the icy skull-cap of the planet Earth.
How lofty, how pure are thy cold-conceived edges.

Icebergs, Icebergs, back of the North-Atlantic, august
    Buddhas
frozen on uncontemplated seas, glittering lighthouses of
sterile Death, the bewildered cry of silence is age-enduring.

Icebergs, Icebergs, self-sufficing hermits, confined coun-
    tries,
far away and free of vermin.
Progenitors of the islands, progenitors of the water-
    springs
seeing you, knowing you my intimates. . . .

Old Age

Evenings! Evenings! How many evenings for one single
    morning!
Scattered islets, bodies of cast-iron, shells!
A thousand-strong we stretch upon his bed, fatal disorder!

Age, vigil-keeper, memories: waste lands of melancholy!
Useless tackle, slow dismemberment!
So already come our marching orders!
Pushed off! To quit pushed off!
Leaden-hued descent with mist behind . . .
and the pale wake of leaving still Unknowing.

LOUIS ARAGON

Louis Aragon, born 1898 *near Toulon. Took part in the First World War as an ‘aide-chirurgien’. With André Breton and Paul Éluard he initiated the surrealist movement about* 1924-25. *The former he had met in the Hôpital du Val de Grâce in Paris—Breton being a psychiatrist—and shared his outlook of intellectual revolt against outmoded academic values not only in writing but also in the realms of thought and assessment of life. In* 1929 *occurred a political schism between them. Aragon became more and more active in the cultural field of communism. He participated, for example, in the International Congress of Writers at Kharkov in* 1930 *; in* 1935*—the fascist ‘war’ having begun—he was active as a member of the International Congress of Writers in Defence of Culture. Aragon, J.-R. Bloch, Jean Cassou, Tristan Tzara, André Malraux* (*the writer and producer of the film* Espoir—Days of Hope) *all fought for the Spanish Republicans. Aragon and Bloch were editors of* Ce Soir *and in the days of Liberation Aragon was still editor. He had been through the Dunkirk retreat in a medical capacity, and he continued to fight with his pen under the name of François Lacolère. Apart from clandestine writings, appeared the famous* Crève-Cœur, *followed by* Les Yeux d'Elsa (*Elsa being his wife, Elsa Triolet, the authoress of* Le Premier Accroc, Coûte Deux Cents Francs, *awarded* Le Prix Goncourt). *Lately he has published a novel,* Aurélien, *and then* La Diane Française.*

He has always been greatly interested in the theory of versification. Although he does not subscribe to many of the French traditional rules (*e.g. alternating feminine and masculine rhymes*), *he has an innate lyricism which links up with Hugo, who in his time had also brought many innovations into French poetry.*

Elsa

So deep your eyes that as I lean to drink
Their pools the light of all the suns reflect
Lovers in despair plunge from their brink
So deep I lose the power to recollect

87

Now beneath black wings the ocean heaves
Then sunshine in your eyes and gone the scorn
June clouds are shaken from an angel's sleeves
Never more blue the sky than over corn

The winds dispel the heaven's wrath in vain
Your eyes are still more bright when tears they lodge
The very sky is jealous of their rain
No glass so blue as at the fragments' edge

Mother of Seven Sorrows tear-drenched rays
Seven swords have pierced the prisms gaily painted
For dawns where tears have flown bring sharper days
Bluer the iris when with grief acquainted

Your eyes in sorrow made a double rent
Where through the miracle of the Kings was seen
As by the manger head in reverence bent
They saw the mantle of our Blessèd Queen

One pair of lips in May can voice the airs
Of all the songs and breathe each sad *alas*
Yet heaven's too small for all the million stars
Lacking your eyes to speak for all that was

Child gazing in his picture-book wide-eyed
Imagination fastened by its power
Your open eyes who knows if they have lied
Wild flowers expanding after April shower

What hidden lightning from those beds may stab
O lavender where insects rape their prey
I am at the mercy of the weaving web
A sailor drowning in mid-August sea

I have searched pitch-blende where radium lies
My fingers burned at the forbidden fire
Yet I have rediscovered Paradise
Here in your eyes Peru-Golconda of desire

And then one night befell the Crack of Doom
Amid the reefs the wreckers set alight
I saw above the waves in Stygian gloom
Your eyes your eyes O Elsa gleaming bright

The Night of May

The spectres shunned the way that was my way
But field-clinging mists betrayed their breath
Night hung lightly with the plain beneath
When we had left the walls of La Bassée

A farm-fire is flaming in this desert where
Silence is huddled by the road-ditch weeds
A plane hovers above and tells its beads
A flare suspending over Saint-Nazaire

How tracks a hundred times recrossed can harass
These poor lost ghosts and thus derange their reason
Plumes of panic mount on the horizon
Above houses a prey to the tanks of Arras

Disturber of two wars you I behold
Here the hill and here the necropolis
Darkness adds darkness to an orphaned darkness
Shadows of to-day to shadows old

We who dreamed in the uncrowned grasses once
The earth a hole dateless with no *Here Lies*
Shall we be born in your mythologies
But the official guide no longer drones

Blue ghosts of Vimy twenty years have trod
See how I the propeller-path of dawn
Dare around this obelisk to turn
Here where you slumber ill so ill-bestowed

Must pain before your eyes for ever pass
No rest for heroes and who cried *we are none*
At the new shock from the gun *False Trianon*
From the true calvary with its verdant grass

The dead the living trembling can dissemble
The living dead who have but sleep assumed
To-night the living find themselves exhumed
Trembling the dead the disinterred resemble

Has darkest night before so banished day
O Musset where your Muse and where your haunts
Here in these precincts rise laburnum scents
Year Nineteen-forty the night the *Night of May*

The Night of Dunkirk

France like a stuff our feet have worn and frayed
Has bit by bit refused to bear our tread

Where in the tide weed-woven corpses lift
The boats capsized like Bishops' bonnets lift

Here ends a camp a hundred thousand strong
And Malo beach the sea and sky prolong

Beneath this night where rot the horses slain
Hooves of migratory herds beat in my brain

The level-crossing opens—we depart
To re-discover our unsorted heart

A thousand loves throb in John Lackland's breast
Will they at last a thousand times find rest

O arrow-piercèd Saint Sebastian
How much how much your fate resembles mine

Assured that they will hear who weakness had
To spare their own and soothe the heart that bled

I at least this confessed love shall cry
Whose flames arising pattern 'gainst the sky

My cries my cries shall shake the burning town
Somnambulists from roofs shall topple down

My cries of love shall in your head resound
The Knives O Knives of grinder on his round

My cries my cries in every ear shall ring
O where are you my Sight my precious thing

My cries my cries louder than cannon-shot
Louder than wounded men or drunken sot

My cries will say Your lips are beakers where
I drink the long red draught of love-despair

Your ivy-twining arms can hold me yet
I cannot die—for those who die forget

Could I forget the eyes of those who went
Forget Dunkirk—the lover's last lament

I cannot sleep as lights flash in and out
Who could forget the wine of drunken bout

Soldiers have dug their narrow six-foot room
And seem to try the shadow of the tomb

Flintlike faces crazed defiant air
Their slumber is a prescient despair

The scents of Spring this sand has never known
And May is dying in this Northern Dune

Tears are Alike

A grey heaven is peopled with angels of faience
Grey that a pent-up sorrow saddens
It tells of tearful days of Mayence
The Rhine is dark where weep the Rhine-maidens

Sometimes we found in a narrow alley
A soldier stabbed and in the dust
Sometimes a peace that did not tally
With the gentle hills where the vine-shoots thrust

I have drunk distillation of cherries
I have drunk oaths exchanged under the breath
The churches palaces had the beauty of fairies
To me at twenty whose senses were deaf

What did I know of war or defeat
The love of France being a love forbidden
When the voice we hear is the voice of false prophet
Can that resurrect a hope long-hidden

I remember the songs of sorrow
I remember the signs on the wall
Chalked at night to be seen the morrow
I could not decipher the cryptic scrawl

Who can to memory assign a start
Say how things present into future taper
Where past or ballad join or part
When misery is but a yellowing paper

Like those of awakened child in bed
Blue eyes of the conquered trouble our peace
The relieving squad with iron tread
Shivers the river's silences

Plaint for the Great Eclipse
of France

If there could be a quire of viols veiled
Within our heart a fire that nought could quench
The eclipse to tell and our dear love of France
Might there be still a night where no stars paled
Might there be still

If night be fine the shadows will relate
As blind-man holds the strings but does not know
The instrument nor tones the sky may show
Let us intone imprisoned in this drear set
Let us intone

This is the theme that I take up anew
The very same of Love O phlogiston
Blind Homer spoke unheard the loveless one
How bright dawn broke though little then they knew
How bright dawn broke

For women ended are love's coloured hours
Their eyes defended by their languorous lids
Sunday or Thursday love no tears forbids
No longer thirsty lost in shadowed towers
No longer thirsty

The shadow of the towers a fire-dial mark
Inscribe the tardy hours of each dull season
Upon the darkened cobbles of the prison
For here time hobbles death a lying clerk
For here time hobbles

Compare the lag the mad whom they intern
The heart which dripped within its fleshly gaol
Can it speak to lags its language frail
The sky which has been dipped in water-cistern
The sky which has been dipped

Has heart sufficient grieved to have you back
Memory scatters leaves in lingering frost
Like a scarecrow arms out crosswise thrust
In hands that sow oblivion bends the stalk
Oblivion bends the stalk

The months less urgent see the heart derail
But Spring resurgent for me will ever sigh
Words of another May but in love's eye
The wall will ever stay though flowers assail
Will ever stay
The dead who died in May

Song of Faith

We shall smell again the wood-fires that burn
We shall feel the stir of the wind soft as feather
Once more as of old our maidens will yearn
To waltz in the meads to the tune of fair weather
Heralds once more of Spring's fresh return

Queens of the Twilight these songs intoxicate
As the reluctant sun withdraws from the scenes
Your cheeks bear the sanguine blush of her palette
The night comes tardily with her violins
And lingering evening culls the violet

Desire in Spring with amorous thoughts plays dice
No sleep but is haunted with romantic strains
We live sleepless days possessed by lunacies
Love's maddening philtre courses through our veins
The playful boy runs off with blindfold eyes

The crazed with old secrets will rejuvenate the earth
So long as the gorse regains its golden glow
And when my lusty limbs feel the flowers breathe
Is it not Tristan embracing his Yseult
For the tenderness of love is a freshly-twined wreath

Each will have his music each beguiling bliss
The magic of April whispers to my senses
Murmuring soft words that melt to wantonness
And I am pervaded having no defences
With unforgettable forgetfulness

G   97

Carved names of lovers their fate may foretell
Hearts speak their hopes to the listening bough
Dreams write in the mirror what a breath may dispel
On the shadowy kiss the ghost of a vow
Or in the transfixed hearts scratched on the well

Happy pairs who love where the river springs
See on its surface the May-flies in flight
Surprise in the reeds the tale the wind brings
And as once in his garden Perceval the knight
Listens at ease to the birds' jargonings

Richard Cœur-de-Lion

If the universe a barrack-room resembles
Here in French Touraine where you and I are penned
If invading foot our field of lucerne tramples
If dawn today will never find an end

Must I on my fingers account each hour and minute
Must I hate myself who never yet had hated
A stranger to my heart who finds no haven in it
This my country—MINE—who wonders that I doubted

I who may not watch the swallow flying over
Speaking to the heavens in songs that are forbidden
Even the passing cloud has been my base deceiver
Betraying as it brings lost dreams we should have hidden

Thought may in words no longer dare expression
No lips murmur more the old songs of come-hither
Silence itself becomes an indiscretion
Where sun is to be feared as much as foul weather

They are brute strength we are but the number
Those who suffer here the more to us belong
Their efforts are in vain to make our night more sombre
The prisoner himself composes his own song

Song pure as the rill which cheers the mountain-ranger
White like the bread we ate in far-off days
A song climbing high above an ancient manger
Where up aloft it meets the shepherd's gaze

Shepherd sailor carter venerable confessor
Steel or clothmaker word-coiner penny-liner
Business and tradesmen market-woman wise professor
Telegraph-wire repairer butcher coal-grimed miner

French of every name questing like your Blondel
Howsoever fate our ways has joined or parted
Hear whispers of freedom in the hopeful rondel
Sung from his prison by Richard Lion-Hearted

More Beautiful than Tears

Some people find me too alive it seems
I bring to life discomforting remorse
My brazen rhymes disturb their quiet dreams
With noises that would galvanise a corpse

If grinding tanks should dislocate my verse
If shrill axle cries are far from pleasant
The angel-stops gave way to thunder's curse
And Dunkirk's memory is ever present

In doubtful taste agreed but this is War
And some of us in taste are pretty queer
And in our nostrils clings its acrid char
And some of us got drunk on Brussels beer

I speak of love and then my love displeases
When all is fine for me it rains for you
You say my meadows have too many daisies
My night too many stars my sky's too blue

As probes the heart-dissecting medico
Among my words for cheap effects you pried
Have I not seen Pont Neuf and Louvre go
Will vengeance leave you still unsatisfied

You may enslave the sea-gull on the wing
You may condemn the poet to be dumb
But take the poet's right his France to sing
And you will try in vain till kingdom come

France fair maid who visitest each door
If ever I forget let it be told
Your eyes are like the sheaves of flowers you bore
Which starred your apron in the Springs of old

Could our love be feigned our passion false
Smile on this brow this sky cloud-torn and grey
The understanding smile of County Beauce
Catching the poppied corn on Summer day

Have not her arms the beauty statues have
Here in this land of stone of golden bread
The sweet perfection all her sons can give
Watched by Jean Racine's eternal shade

At Rheims the angel smiles with perfect lips
A glimpse of sun seen at its fair decline
What sure damnation saint or prophet sips
Before that hair so redolent of wine

Ingres of Montauban in purest line
The hollow of her shoulder drew wherein
Lingers the long desire as rocks refine
The peaty water of the mountain burn

O Laura he had loved your later peer
Her for whom murdered we bleed today
Petrarch whom inspired like pointed spear
The doe who from the huntsmen sped away

Evoke Evoke so that the ghosts find haven
The mirage of Arabian-night décor
The murals of St. John to Brantôme's cavern
From Roncevaux to hillsides of Vercors

Dream-laden winds from Arles were never harsh
Their dreams too deep for heart to put in words
When in Aunis-Saintonge the yellow marsh
Is churned by tanks of ruthless conquering hordes

In tournament each province city town
Vies with the other in their names and flings
Those flowery garlands like a challenge down
That dream and reason in confusion brings

O chains which barred the sky and you Durance
O land of shepherds coloured like your fruit
Manosque so loved by François King of France
That on the Arab walls her name he wrote

Belovèd madcap jealous without cause
Who fail to recognise yourself in these
My lines—on Naurouze' brow awhile we pause
Our double fate must choose between two seas

No—like a song that lingers in the brain
You wish to haunt again the Mont Ventoux
The Seine flows gently here and Lamartine
Dreams of his Madeleine in the orchard row

Woman wine and cradle-song of old
Or scene my wit is slow to celebrate
Are not these fecund breasts and limbs of gold
Like pines and Brittany like suns that set

Breastplate of white where burn my lips with fire
Cider milk of joy satiety
Would not soldiers exiled in Palmyre
Die for their loved and secret Normandy

How should I guess what all these charms beget
These names of flesh and blood like Andelys
The image turns and then our cheeks are wet
With tears—stay mute O Paris Paris

Paris home of songs of sudden ire
Whose banners lately overwashed must fade
Metropolis as bright as Polar-star
True Paris only at the barricades

Paris of civil-strife of Cours-la-Reine
Of Blancs-Manteaux of bitter February skies
From Saint-Antoine to hill slopes of Suresnes
Paris heart-rending as a glazier's cries

Flee these grim outskirts where all troubles start
Dawn follows dawn as life flows sadly on
The Oise has lost her charm the Marne her heart
Valois deserted with her Sylvie gone *

Ramparts of memory we man
With twenty-year-old prayers where clouds have frowned
Moulin de Laffaux—Chemin des Dames
Pilgrim do not forget the battleground

Over dusty plains your feet move on
Pursuing without pause and undismayed
Over the Meuse and forested Argonne
The dawn of immortal glory but betrayed

* *Translator's note.*—Reference to Parc de Sylvie at Chantilly. Théophile de Viau wrote a poem *Maison de Sylvie* in honour of la duchesse de Montmorency.

Like the wounded hind a coward struck
The pond's blue eye broods over gold-flecked bowers
Halt on the fleeing exile's mountain-track
In Courbet's land where mandragora flowers

Lost is Alsace where when the Rhine o'erflows
From frozen branches drop inert the pheasants
Where Werther for a moment quits his woes
To revel with the merry-making peasants

The storm may rage from Dunkirk to Port-Vendre
But voices so beloved can never drown
None has the power to still the tales that wander
Around Ardennes of Aymon's sons' renown

Who from our ears could drive this flute-refrain
Which from our throats for centuries arose
O youthful throng who sang *La Marjolaine*
"The laurels are cut down . . ." and soon our foes

For now with beat of hooves the forest rings
My brimming heart wells over at the source
Hope speaks at night the language of the springs
Duguesclin comes thundering on his horse

What matter if I die before is seen
The sacred brow which patient waits above
"Dance on my child Dance capucine"
My country is my hunger want and love.

The Night of July

A strange perfume deep and sad
An illusion of roses above my head

No it is not the day nor is it the rose
This motet of motors in monotone morose

Nor is it the skylark this night in July
Where searchlights blink their chilly eye

In vain I say Sleep I cannot but know
That a fire afar is gilding my window

The shadow has more secrets than water's green heart
And watchers with their lanterns sometimes start

Up the birds affright owls in the dark
And it is not the dawn nor is it the lark

No longer a need to fix the moment
When nights have no lovers with love itself absent

Will dawn break for a skylark's trill
For love sufficed once a nightingale

But the day I tell of has a dearer price
The nightingale must break the silences

Am I dreaming still or burns the sky
For in the wind strange phrases fly

Like the sobs of Naples in the breeze
With Nicola Porpora at the organ-keys

The soft speech of fishermen in their bark
The soft speech of Laura and of Petrarch

The speech of Tasso and the lowly
Of Thomas Aquinas St. Francis the Holy

That Othello at Venice spoke to Desdemona
That violins sobbed in the air of Cremona

Miraculous phrases fused into one
Thoughts of Palladio expressed in stone

What the Siennese shadows magic mellow
Said in hot evenings to Uccello

Italian words which welcome give
To the rhyme of freedom this Summer eve

For this night is ever Michelangelo's
As dawn-fingered hope tears the veil of rose

The black flower shudders what Angelus
Clears the mountains sweeps sorrows from the roofs

The excited soul in ecstatic grace
Is it the White Peace of Cumes on the Brenner Pass

Is it the White Peace emerging from the fire
This roar is it Leopardi's ire

Who could disentangle these distant cries
A world in childbirth or a world which dies

For every creature of this earth
Cries alike in death and alike in birth

What do they say what names re-live
That to thin blood rich wine can give

Gramsci Matteoti.   No kingly throne
Nor songs for cross—a torch alone—

In memory of the heart versed and quick
His people's grammar and arithmetic

Gramsci Matteoti sing above Italy's doom
Nothing lost or forgot in martyrdom

Latin words in grave carillon
Gramsci Matteoti a matin-song

O Italy long in tortured throes
The Lipari isles will return your heroes

Now July again when teeth are aglint
July the month when Bastilles are burnt

The roses of old explain their gleams
By this couch-grass the Lictors set in flames

At last fire is set to the public fair
Which burns itself out in the gravelled pyre

The carnival of Rome aged a score
Caesar decrees rain nor fine weather more

The clown the juggler dancer on his rope
Crying God a' mercy all run up

On the bells of his chariot hangs Phaeton false lord
And the sand is strewn with marks of pasteboard

The equilibrist falls and the swallower of tow
Flames with the sword-swallower as he falls below

And while the people his greatness feel
And in their circus tyrants fall under his heel

The stallion Liberty tears through the screen
Dante rises from Hell and the stars are seen.

Printed in Great Britain
at Hopetoun Street, Edinburgh,
by T. and A. CONSTABLE LTD.
Printers to the University of Edinburgh